How to Be a Smart SOB Like Me

How to Be a Smart SOB Like Me

Larry Landgraf

Fresh Ink Group
Roanoke

How to Be a Smart SOB Like Me

Copyright © 2016
by Larry Landgraf
All rights reserved

Fresh Ink Group
An Imprint of:
The Fresh Ink Group, LLC
PO Box 525
Roanoke, TX 76262
Email: info@FreshInkGroup.com
www.FreshInkGroup.com

Edition 1.0   2012
Edition 2.0   2017

Book design by Ann E. Stewart / FIG

Cover design by Stephen Geez / FIG

Except as permitted under the U.S. Copyright Act of 1976, no part of this publication may be reproduced, distributed, or transmitted in any form or by any means, or stored in a database or retrieval system, without prior written permission of the Fresh Ink Group, LLC.

BISAC Subject Headings:
BIO000000 **BIOGRAPHY & AUTOBIOGRAPHY** / General
BIO026000 **BIOGRAPHY & AUTOBIOGRAPHY** / Personal Memoirs
PHI034000 **PHILOSOPHY** / Social

Library of Congress Control Number: 2017932195

Paper-cover ISBN-13: 978-1-936442-51-5
Hardcover ISBN-13: 978-1-936442-50-8
Ebook ISBN-13: 978-1-936442-52-2

Table of Contents

Introduction 1

1. Work and Employment 9
2. Learning, Gardening, Fruit, and Trees 15
3. College, Reading, and Mental Strength 22
4. Language and Succeeding 27
5. Around the Ranch (The Early Years) 30
6. More Around the Ranch 41
7. Still on the Ranch 46
8. Rockport and Playing 55
9. 6th, 7th, and 8th Grades 61
10. High School 66
11. Flooding 77
12. Book Knowledge and Summer Jobs 82
13. Plants 92
14. Birds and Animals 99
15. Typing, Bookkeeping, and English 110
16. Kingsville and Early Shrimping 114
17. Shrimping 122
18. Salesman 146
19. New House 151
20. Tank Accident 162
21. Poker 169
22. Iceland 175
23. Traveling, Sumy, and E. 180
24. Las Vegas 190
25. Overcrowding and Space 195
26. Religion 204

27. Politics	208
28. Economy and Warmongering	215
29. Government	221
30. Respect	227
31. Surviving	231
32. Financial Planning and Having Fun	237

Epilogue	242
About the Author	246

Introduction

A few days ago, I was watching the Weather Channel on TV, and a weatherman was asking some people on the street some very simple questions. One question was "in which direction does the sun rise and set?" A few people could not answer this question. Another question was "can you name the four seasons?" Several people could not answer this question either! Now I thought to myself, "damn, those are some really dumb people!" In my opinion, there should not be a single person on this planet who cannot answer these basic questions, but the fact is, there are probably a lot of people who cannot answer these and many, many more very simple questions. These are important things everyone should learn as they grow up. These people were walking down the street, and appeared to be ordinary people, functioning in life like everyone else, putting one foot in front of the other, but in reality maybe their brains were in overload just getting one foot in front of the other, and they were, in fact, on the verge of literally falling flat on their faces. Can these people learn more and function better? I think yes. That is what gave me the idea of writing this book.

Why the SOB in the title of this book? Well, mainly to catch your eye, but also because for too many people I'm sure, the title SOB fits me very well, especially if you happen to work in any form of government, and especially the Texas Parks and Wildlife Department (TP&WD). If you read my last book, *Dangerous Waters,* you will know why I say this. It really doesn't matter if you read that book though, what matters is that you read this book. *Dangerous Waters* was written to help me; this book is to help *you.*

If you don't think I'm an SOB now, I'm sure many of you will certainly think so by the time you finish this book; maybe long before you finish. Some of you may get so pissed off at me before you get to the end, you don't even finish the book. That will hurt you, not me. I may say some things which will offend you, but remember I am trying to help you. Do I care what you think about me? No, certainly not. I really don't care what other people think about me, and you should not care what other people think about you either. I am what I am, I am who I am, and if you don't like it, well then, you can kiss my fat ass! I don't care what you think. If you care what other people think about you, then other people will change you. You will not change me. Even if you slam this book shut right now and throw it away, you will have at least experienced lesson #1. Don't care about the other 347 lessons? That's your choice.

If I don't fit your profile of what a normal person should be, then screw you. First of all, I have never claimed to be normal. In fact, I don't think I have ever considered myself as normal, and that has never been a goal of mine. I have always strived to be just me, whatever that may be, but normal, no! I am an individual and unique, and think I have always been so. I will never conform to what you think is normal and I will never be a card carrying member of *A Nation of Sheep*. This was one of the few books I read while in High School that influenced my life. I am constantly evolving, but in a direction which suits me, not you. I don't think I'm crazy or nuts, but will not entirely rule that out either.

I was taught by my parents when I was young, that I should not tell anyone everything I know. I was told that would make them smarter than me, as they would then know everything they know and everything I know. Now, I don't think this makes any sense, and it certainly doesn't make any difference to me. Frankly, I just don't care how smart you are or can become. I just hope I can avoid being killed or injured, by some stupid person doing something really stupid. If I can help make more people less stupid, maybe I will have a better chance of living a little bit longer. I may be able to help you become a little smarter, but probably not less stupid. I've heard stupid is for forever, and this is probably true. But maybe if you are a little smarter, which I can help you with, you will think a little more before you act. This, in turn, will hopefully make you do less stupid things. Try it and see if it works. There are way too many stupid people out there. I know; I see them on the highway every time I go somewhere.

I do not know why my parents told me not to tell people too much. Maybe they were just trying to shut me up. Kids learn very early to ask "why?" Maybe I was always telling them stuff and asking too many questions, and they just wanted to get rid of me. Kids really do ask a lot of seemingly silly questions, but this is the way they learn. I didn't get all the answers, but I did ask. Maybe some or even a lot of kids don't, or can't, ask all that many questions. That's just too bad, as this is how you have to learn when you are too young to read well, and you can't really do much else.

Learning to walk is a challenge, and learning to get around the house, yard and then the neighborhood can be challenging too when you are young. There always has to be some help from parents, relatives and siblings, or you will not learn what you need to learn before you get into school. Maybe some parents are not smart enough to answer the questions the kids are asking, or are too busy to raise the kids who are their responsibility to rear to the best of their ability. This can be a serious problem. If you are a parent, take the time to teach your kids all you can. This is your job; your responsibility. If kids do not ask questions and get answers, they cannot learn. Parents should know this. Parents must be willing to answer the questions. If your life is so busy, why do you have kids? You must make time for them. I suspect too many people have not made time for their kids, and this is really sad, as now there are a lot of dumb people as a result.

What will the next generation of kids be like? This can create a vicious cycle for perpetuating dumb people. It doesn't have to be this way though. I found other ways of learning. How about you? Considering all the dumb people around, someone needs to help these poor souls. I cannot replace your parents, but I am going to try to tell you everything I know, though this will be impossible, and you may already know some of the things I will cover, but it never hurts to repeat. I will also tell some pretty good stories about my life as I go, and share my beliefs and frustrations, all with a good measure of sarcasm and a little humor too. You will get some insight into my life and why I do things. I will also try to give you the strength you need to make better decisions, and get you started down a path which will lead to better finances, more happiness and hopefully to a better life, which will lead you to a greater respect for yourself and those around you. I will try to motivate you, and show you there is hope despite your parents, and it is never too late to learn, but you have to be willing to learn. I will help as much as I can, and maybe, just maybe, helping some dumbass to smarten up a bit, will save me from one of his or her stupid mistakes. That is my goal.

If you have a college degree, are living a good life and are happy with your life, this book is probably not for you. If you are mentally stable, know what you want out of life and are working in the direction of improving your life, then you probably do not need this book, but maybe this book can still help you a little anyway. I expect you will learn a few things you did not know before, and you might also find an interesting story or two along the way, as this book is also an autobiography of my life, with a lot of pretty good stories about as much of my life I can remember. I believe you will be glad you read the book, even if you really did not need it. I'm also sure you probably know someone this book can help, and maybe you might want to buy a copy to help him or her out a little. Maybe this book will save you from your dumb friends, and the stupid things they do. Think about that.

If on the other hand, you are not happy, if you are not moving forward with your life, if you do not know where your life is headed, you may really need a helping hand, and that is what this book is, a helping hand. Maybe your kids do not listen to you, as few teenagers do. Maybe you need to try to get them to read this book, if you can. This book is for anyone stuck in a rut and needing direction. Everyone knows someone like this, and even if this book cannot help you, give a copy to someone you care about, so you can help them. You will be glad you did.

At some point in your life, there will be someone who will touch your life and heart, if you will just let them. This person for me was my older sister. I was pretty sickly when I was young, and brought home almost every childhood disease that came my way. My older sister didn't miss a day of school the first five years, and this is when I started school. I brought home the measles, mumps, chicken pox and everything else I could catch. I brought these diseases home, and gave them to the entire family. I was one to share with everyone when I was that age. I had measles and chicken pox at the same time, and was pretty sick. My older sister bought a book for me to read. This book was *Tom Sawyer*. I loved the book, and it really touched my life. The character also pretty much describes me, the first fifteen years of my life —barefoot, wild and free. I think this also describes me fairly well now.

When I was about nine years old, I had my tonsils taken out. Afterwards, I don't think I caught even a cold for the next ten years. I was never sick anymore, and though I plainly remember having my tonsils taken out, and it was extremely painful, I am very glad they were removed. I'm certain the rest of the family was glad they were gone, as I didn't bring home any more diseases. Tonsils are two little glands in your throat that absorb poisons in your body. I don't think there is any other function for these glands, except to make you sick. I remember being promised all the ice cream I could eat when I got home, but after having these glands cut out, as much as my throat hurt, the last thing I wanted was ice cream. I had a hard time swallowing, and didn't want to eat anything. Swallowing is also a reflex action. I remember, the harder I tried to not swallow, the more I seemed to do exactly that.

When I grew up and started school, I asked a lot fewer questions at home. I began learning in school, and outside of class I began to learn by doing. I believe learning by doing is the best way to learn, and you will of course make many mistakes along the way. But as time goes on, you will hopefully try harder to achieve what you are trying to do, and learn more and retain more in the process. You can't forget learning in school though. Studying hard is your job in life so far. Learning in school, along with learning by doing outside of school, if you put forth the effort to learn things which will help you in life, you will grow up capable of taking care of yourself and a family, should you choose to have one. Too many people try to raise a family when they are not equipped to do so, either financially or mentally, or both.

To start your education, let me tell you the sun always rises in the east and sets in the west, more or less anyway. The four seasons are winter, spring, summer and fall (or autumn). It is hard for me to believe there are people who do not know this. The good news is you are not one of them anymore. The sun is approximately 93 million miles from Earth, and Earth is the third planet from the sun, Mercury being the closest planet to the sun and Venus being the second. I certainly hope you know winter is the cold time of the year, and summer is the hot time of the year. The northern half of Earth, the northern hemisphere, will be experiencing winter at the same time the southern hemisphere, the southern half, will be experiencing summer. The northern hemisphere is separated from the southern hemisphere by the equator. Spring and fall are transitional seasons, spring advancing into summer and fall advancing into winter.

Now, let's move on to some things I am not going to teach you. I will not teach you how to hot wire a car, cheat on exams, rob a bank, do drugs, pick a lock, hold up a convenience store, or any crap like that. If these are some of the things you do best, you should seriously rethink your life. If you spend much of your life in front of the boob tube, spend much of your time with your home boys, or just out in the streets feeling alone and rejected, you have no life and should seriously consider getting one. I never knew anyone who said they wanted to grow up to be a loser, but there were many in the past who I can only classify as thugs, who had to know the path they were heading down, and maybe they really did want to grow up to be losers. They were at least doing all the wrong things, but I think they only lacked direction. No one ever told them, or showed them the direction they should be going. They never had anyone touch their lives, and they were left behind.

When kids are young, they need spankings. Spanking kids will not kill them. I'm not talking about beating them, I'm talking about spanking. You cannot reason with kids with words, and spanking is the only good alternative to help guide kids down the path towards learning respect. Spankings must be dealt with a generous supply of love for them to work well. Kids are born with a conscience, but the conscience is a sleeper cell. Spanking, when deserved, will help wake up this sleeper cell, so it can help guide your kids down a path in life which will keep them out of trouble. Spanking may not be appropriate for older kids, but stern direction is mandatory. Kids need to be taught life is not free, and they must be introduced to work, and must learn responsibility. There must also be punishment for not adhering to the strict rules they must learn, to keep them out of trouble. The problem is there are too many weak parents or single parents, who cannot or will not guide, punish, and push their children down good life paths. This is sad; not only for the parents, but for the kids and everyone whose lives they touch.

There are always solutions to any of the problems you might have, regardless of your age. You just need to search them out. If you are going nowhere in life, maybe you just need to go to the local police department, and tell them you have no place to go and need help to try to build a new life for yourself. Ask them where you can get the help you need. They say their job is "to protect and serve". Hold them to this. If they cannot help you, which I seriously doubt would be the case, don't give up. Go to the county courthouse. Try the sheriff's office, or a county judge, or go to the Department of Human Services. Whatever you do though, get the help you need, and don't stop until you do. When you find someone who will help you, follow their instructions, put your nose to the grindstone and work hard for a new life. All too many people don't want to work for what they can get out of life. Don't be one of these people. The good things in life require hard work. Working hard is a mandatory requirement and will not kill you.

The first stop may not solve your problems, and if you are not willing to put forth all the necessary effort, nothing will improve. All too many people let their egos get in the way, and never ask for help. We're talking about your life here. Are you going to let an ego screw up the rest of your life? I think one thing that helped me a lot, is I never thought I could fail. Failure was never an option, and failure never crossed my mind. Well, maybe it crossed my mind a few times, but I put forth the effort, whatever was necessary, so failure was not possible. I do not know exactly how I learned this, but that I was always willing and able to work at achieving whatever I wanted to do. I studied hard and worked hard, learning all that was necessary to achieve everything I wanted out of life. You can do this too, no matter where you start. I had many setbacks, and I even started over a couple times, but one thing I never did was give up, and you must not give up either if you want to succeed.

There are a few things everyone should be doing and learning to have a comfortable, productive, and rewarding life. The most important things in life are the rewards that are earned, not the rewards you can take at someone else's expense. Life is short and should be fun and rewarding. It cannot be fun and rewarding if you are dumb, broke, in jail or prison, out on the street, and you have no family or friends. Cellmates will never be friends. Learn to do new things by DOING, and if you have to read a little along the way, then do the reading and studying necessary to get the job done. You may not always do it right the first time, but over time you will learn to do things better and better. Always be punctual and always do what you say you will do. People will not tolerate you if you are consistently late, and if they cannot depend on you. Look toward finding things to do which will make your life better and act responsibly, not things that will land you in prison and really f_#% up your life. Do you know what I'm saying?

Chapter 1
Work and Employment

Let's say you are out on the street and have nothing. The good news is, you only have one place to go, and that is up. If you have no place to stay, no money, no job and nothing to do, you have to start doing something. Clean up the trash on the streets if you need to, just to be doing something. This will give you exercise, and maybe someone will notice what you are doing, and give you some help. If not, then don't worry about it. Open doors for people at places of business, especially restaurants, and give them a little bow. Say hi to people you see, and remember to smile. Just keep doing things for people, and be nice and courteous. Sooner or later, someone will notice. But, if no one ever lifts a finger to help you, you can't worry about it. Just being nice and courteous does not always work, but it's worth a try. Being pleasant to others is good practice for life, especially if you are working for an employer, but also if you are unemployed and looking for work. Never just be idle. Always try to be doing something, whether you are getting paid for it or not.

Look around to see what kind of businesses are in your area. Pick up any trash you might see around the buildings, and keep your eye out for any chores you can do for these businesses. Ask the business owner, and any other people who may live in the area, for small jobs you are capable of handling. Usually there are a few people around, who will give you small jobs. There may not be much pay involved, but a job is a job. Maybe there is simple painting, or sweeping and mopping jobs, for which the owner can provide you with the tools and materials you will need. Never just ask for money, as this will label you as a bum, and bums go nowhere. Help yes, but money never, but don't turn it down if someone should offer. I can't stress enough how important honesty and integrity are. Always be totally honest, and do all jobs to the best of your ability, and don't be messy and make a bigger problem with your work. Remember, small jobs can lead to bigger and better jobs, and the better you do the small jobs, the faster someone will notice and possibly offer you some bigger and higher paying jobs. There is a saying, if you want something done right, you must do it yourself. Find out exactly what your employer wants, and how he or she wants it done, and do your very best to do the job exactly like they want it done. Try to do the job as if they had done it themselves.

Also, look at yourself and how you are dressed, and how clean you are. Maybe you can't do a lot about this, but do the best you can to look better. Is there a Goodwill Store around? They can help with clothes. Reasonably short hair is always a plus, and a clean shave, for you guys, if you can. People generally don't like dirty people, and associate dirty people with thieves, bums and thugs and they will avoid you. Looking better will go a long way towards helping you get ahead. This goes for you gals too. Dress appropriately for the job at hand. Especially important is to not stink. Keep your body odor under control.

As you inch ahead, invest in yourself as much as you are able, and don't expect to do more than inch ahead. Also, never get discouraged, and be forever optimistic. A good and pleasant attitude is important, and will go a long way in helping you get ahead faster. People do not like rude and nasty people, and will avoid you like the plague. If you are on any drugs or alcohol, quit. People can generally tell, and you will go nowhere in your search for work. Never use foul language either. This will get the door slammed in your face quicker than just about anything. And always be gracious when you are turned down as well. Being nasty when you are turned down will always close that door to you permanently. If you can't stay sober, or follow these simple rules, then I have no pity for you. You are not trying to help yourself, and I would not lift a finger to help you, and neither will anyone else. You are hopeless and may as well be dead.

For you teens and young adults out there, let's say you are still home with your parents. You are the luckiest ones of all, even though you may not realize it. You have your whole life ahead of you, and you may not know where you are going or even which direction to head out in, but at least you have a roof over your head and food to eat. This is an important time in your life, and though you may be too immature and not be equipped to do so, you need to make a lot of choices. You really need to think about your future, and make the correct choices, or you can really screw up the rest of your life. Kids like to have fun, and most kids will exert most of their efforts to have as much fun as they can, and that is normal. You probably won't listen to anyone else, and that is usually common among teenagers, but you had better listen to that little voice inside you, which tells you the difference between right and wrong. You can destroy your life, and the lives of others, in an instant with one bad decision, especially if your life involves drugs, alcohol or violence. Alcohol could have destroyed my life, but I was lucky and it didn't. I never did drugs, though they were readily available, especially through college. I just didn't have a need for them, and you don't either. The alcohol was part of our having fun for too many years, but I was able to get off the booze before it destroyed my life. The sooner you get off alcohol or drugs, the better off you will be. You can't climb the ladder of success, if you are too drunk to even climb, and when you fall, the sudden stop at the bottom of the ladder is very hard and uncomfortable. If you are in school, don't just stay in school, but study like your life depends on it, because it certainly does.

Your school days are the most critical time of your life. The choices you make here, will affect the rest of your life and how much money you will make. Study hard and try to find a part time job, especially during the off season. A part time job will give you the opportunity to learn some additional skills you will need when you get older, like working with your hands, learning to work with people and learning how to respect yourself and respect others. Be sure to make time for your studies though. You will also earn some much needed cash. I worked at a gas or service station learning to service vehicles, pumping gas, cleaning the windshield, and changing flat tires. I also learned to process credit cards and count change. I worked for some local farmers shoveling grain, and hauling the grain to the grain elevators and cutting stalks after the crops were harvested. This was really hot and dirty work, but easily tolerated when you are young and healthy as I was. I even picked cotton, but this task was much tougher than it looked, and this job was short lived.

Hard work builds muscles, and eating foods good for you will also help you down the road. I'm not saying you have to eat perfectly, and only what is good for you, because I never did. I was always at least a little overweight, but never obese except when I was a baby. I burned off most of the baby fat as I grew up. If you are fat, then lose the weight. Being fat will affect the amount of work you can do, and will also affect the jobs you can get and how employers look at you. You should also learn honesty and integrity, if you have not already done so, and how to get along with people. Make customers want to give your boss their repeat business. This can and will directly affect your job. No one likes to do business with places that have poor employees. Poor employees reflect on the business itself. Stand by and do right by your employer, and he will reward you. Don't, and you will be terminated.

There are many, many distractions during your school years that can get you into a lot of trouble. You are learning more about girls, and the fun, but also the problems, they can cause for you. As this book is not just for boys, the same is true for you girls out there. Boys can get you into a lot of trouble, and you do not need to be trying to raise a child, when you should be learning and striving for a good life and a great future. Everyone, boys and girls alike, must learn to say no and stick with it. That goes for not just sex, but alcohol, drugs, drag races, and many, many other mischievous things that are too numerous to name. If you cannot abstain from sex, then at least practice safe sex. Always be prepared. Stay out of trouble, and don't get stuck in menial poverty.

What kind of guy or gal do you want to make your life with after you get out of school? What does your dream guy or dream gal look like? Do you want some fat slob, who has little or no respect for themselves, or anyone else? I don't think so. Well, if you are the fat slob, they do not want you either. Think about that the next time you are pigging out on barbecue, lasagna or whatever you like to pig out on. Lay off the chips and dips, lay off the greasy fried stuff, lay off the monster burgers, lay off the pies and cakes, and definitely lay off the high sugar drinks. If your dream guy or gal is not a pig, then what makes you think they might want you if you are one? They won't and they don't. Of course, if you are a pig and have no intention of changing, there are probably a few pigs of the opposite sex, or even the same sex if that is what you prefer, who might tolerate you, but I don't think anyone can really love a pig. Think about that.

OK let's say you have a job, but it's not going anywhere. With a job you are way ahead of the game. Learn more and work harder, and you will advance further. Even ask your employer what you need to do in order to advance to a higher position with the company. If there is no chance for advancement, then consider changing to another position with another company, at which you can advance. Keep the status quo, and you will be left behind. The money you earn will lose value over time due to inflation, and if your pay is not increasing year after year, you are depreciating and eventually you may even lose your job. The world is advancing, and if you do not continually advance with it, you will be left behind. Believe me, bosses are always looking, and what they are looking for is better people to advance their company. You may not see them looking, but believe me, they will be looking at all their employees. If the economy takes a turn for the worse, the worst employees, and those in positions not truly necessary, will be the first to go. If you are not striving to be better, you will be left behind, and the backsliding does not stop here. If you lose your job, you can't pay your bills. Then you may lose your home, your car, and everything important to you. The next thing you know, you could be out on the streets. Don't let this happen to you. Work hard and always strive to improve, not only yourself, but your job skills too.

If you are unemployed, and there is no job out there for you, then you should think of working for yourself. That is what I did. I learned the skills I needed to be my own employer. This may be a little tougher to do, but if you can find a niche in the market, doing something or making something, then you can get ahead that way. It doesn't have to be an important job; just some type of service job, or some type of job producing something people need or want, and are willing to pay you to do or to produce. If you do find some sort of work to do, then you really need to think of honesty and integrity, which you should always be thinking about, if you want to expect some repeat business. Honesty and integrity are good tools to have, regardless of what you do, and whether or not you are working for yourself or for an employer, and I just can't stress this enough. Keep this in mind throughout your life.

Chapter 2
Learning, Gardening, Fruit and Trees

Learning is something you should be doing your entire life. Learning is very easy when you are young and you have a great capacity for learning, but as you age your mind begins to deteriorate faster and faster, especially if your mind is in idle mode much of the time. When you stop learning, your mind begins to lose more knowledge than it is gaining, and you actually become dumber. You must always strive to learn more than you are losing. I learn many new things every day, and do things to keep my mind active and in the learning mode. Learning is a process where I am aware of my surroundings, sometimes more than at other times, but I am always prepared to learn new things from my daily encounters. You should always be prepared to learn, by paying attention to your surroundings and looking for new things to investigate. An active mind deteriorates much less than an inactive mind.

A good game or two can help keep your mind active, and help to keep the cobwebs out of your head so to speak. I play poker, which keeps my mind active and keeps the numbers and strategies churning in my head. With poker, there are millions of combinations of cards played, and many strategies for playing these cards. The neuro pathways stay active, and this will keep them running smoothly and slows the deterioration process. Alcohol and drugs can speed up the deterioration process significantly.

I now know the difference between an elm tree and a cedar elm tree. I had known they were both elm trees, but just called one of them a broadleaf and the other a small leaf elm. I accidentally learned the name of the cedar elm one day. I did not care enough to know the difference between the two, and never learned, but just stumbled across the name of the cedar elm. That is one method by which you will learn many things. Sycamore and cottonwood trees are very similar. As the result of a dispute, I looked up sycamore tree on the computer and found out what I had thought was a cottonwood tree half my life, was actually a sycamore tree. Live and learn. You may learn some things when they hurt you, or interact with you in some way, and this will happen quite often. You need to pay attention, or you will learn nothing. Your eyes should be wide open at all times, and you should be aware there are many things around you to learn. Always pay attention to what is going on around you, and be prepared to learn something new. You may need to find a dictionary, or encyclopedia or some other reference book, or even take a trip to a local nursery or library to find the answers. Just be aware there are things to learn everywhere, and follow through with learning more about whatever you find interesting. A computer with an internet connection is a wealth of information, and so are the many books and reference materials which can be found in a library. If you want to learn something, there are many cost free places where you can learn.

    The elm tree has large broad leaves with serrated edges, and is a very good shade tree. If you don't know what serrated means, go look it up in the dictionary. The cedar elm is still an elm tree, and has leaves that are basically the same, but are about one fourth the size of the elm leaf. The elm is a fast growing tree, while the cedar elm grows a little slower and does not spread out as much as the elm. The cedar elm doesn't make quite as good a shade tree, but when it gets old enough it can provide good shade. Flooding will not kill elm and cedar elm trees. They grow well in wet areas such as the marsh I live in, on the Guadalupe River delta. They are also disease resistant and easily transplanted, but you need to keep them watered well when transplanting. If you wish to learn the names of the plants growing in your area, the local nursery is a good place to start. Just find the plants in the nursery you have, and look at the name tags as all the plants have name tags. This makes this task very easy, and all you need to do is remember the names. Write them down if you have to. I like to wander around nurseries, just to see all the different varieties of plants available. This little bit of knowledge about the elm trees doesn't make me a genius now, but this little measure of knowledge, and all the other little tidbits I also learned today, will add up over time.

I remember when I was young I was always taking something apart and putting it back together. Sometimes I had a few parts left over, and had to take whatever it was apart over and over several times before I got it back to its original condition, but for the most part I eventually got it back together right. Not always though, and sometimes it didn't work in the first place. Occasionally, I got something working again that did not work when I started. Taking things apart and seeing the inner workings of things, and how they interact with each other to make a working machine, can be very useful in life. You can see how things break, and learn how to replace the broken parts to make them work again. Machines will always break, and to be able to repair these machines, can be very useful around the home. Some people make a lot of money repairing machines for others, who cannot or will not do this task for themselves.

At other times, I was building something from scratch. I did this a lot, and made many things. Some were good and some were not, but it didn't really matter, as I was learning to do things with my hands, and with many of the tools I would use the rest of my life. Learning to do things with your hands is a very good skill to learn. Eventually you will get good at working with your hands, and the endless myriad of hand tools. You may find you have a knack for repairing some things more than others, or you may <u>like</u> repairing something in particular. If you have a choice, stick with repairing the things you like, as that will be more fun. Don't ever say you cannot do something, or you can't use the tools or you are not good with your hands. That is the view of a pessimist. You should always be optimistic. You may need a little more practice to get things done right, but I guarantee you, with practice you will get better. And with enough practice, you will get good. One of my sisters, when we were growing up, would always say "I can't!" and she never did, and never learned to do much of anything. "I can't" never did anything. "I can", will always get things done.

I am learning to be a better gardener, and also working very hard to grow a better orchard. Gardening is simply preparing the soil and fertilizing, planting the seeds and keeping them watered so they will germinate, then mulching and keeping the bugs and weeds out. If you do it wrong, they will not grow well. But do it right and you will have plenty of veggies. This is not a hard task, but it does take some patience and persistence. My orchard includes orange, lemon, nectarine and grapefruit trees, as well as several varieties of plum, peach, apricot, and pear trees. Fruit trees are easily planted. You basically dig a hole in an area where there is sufficient sunlight and stick it in the hole, then add dirt and water. This is a little more difficult this year, as Texas is in one of its worst droughts ever. The year is 2011. Watering is necessary every few days for some of the younger plants and weekly for the larger newly planted plants. The more established trees even need a little extra water. These are simple things, and the things I am learning are not very important to most people, but I am learning and getting some exercise. Always learn and always strive to do things better, and over time you will become a smarter and more productive person. Little things can change your life, and are very rewarding.

Learning to grow fruit is fun, and home grown fruit grown to maturity tastes very good. Commercial fruit is generally picked too green, and not as tasty as when it ripens on the tree. Fruit does not taste the same every year either, as weather conditions can drastically affect the way fruit tastes and its size. There may be pests to deal with that also like the fruit you may grow, and will eat your fruit before it is completely ripe. A little patience and a good gun can take care of the pests, if you can learn to handle a gun properly. And for you animal lovers out there, there is also the option of using live traps. Yes, I do have a live catch trap, and do not just kill everything that comes around. Catch and then release critters a good distance from your property, as they can and will come back if you don't take them far enough away. I like to release the caught critters on the Texas Parks and Wildlife property a few miles away. Let them deal with the pesky critters. Maybe there is a little justice and satisfaction there too.

Some of the fruit trees I grow are citrus. The orange, lemon and grapefruit trees are classified as citrus trees. These trees cannot tolerate too much cold, especially when they are very young. Citrus trees do not lose their leaves during the winter time, and if the weather gets too cold, they will die. They can usually survive a few degrees below freezing, but at some point they will die. The peach, nectarine, plum, apricot, and pear trees on the other hand, can tolerate the cold much better, and will lose their leaves in the winter and actually go dormant. In the spring, these trees will put on new leaves, and bloom to bear fruit when they are mature enough to do so. Most fruit trees will begin to produce a small crop of fruit when they are three or four years old. Most will not produce a large amount of fruit until they are a few years older, and have grown large enough to be able to carry the weight of a large crop of fruit. Most of my fruit trees, as well as shade trees which do not produce fruit go dormant in winter, and will grow new leaves in the spring when it begins to warm up a bit.

I also have one loquat tree. The loquat is a type of Japanese plum, and is a really screwed up tree. It is pretty much an evergreen tree and keeps its leaves the year around. I say pretty much an evergreen tree, because it is not like the pine trees I normally think of when I think of evergreen trees. It has large broad leaves, not needles like the pine trees. It blooms in the fall in our area, rather than the spring like most fruit trees, and the sweet golden yellow fruits of the loquat tree ripen very early in the spring. The loquat fruit has a very large seed in the middle, and there is not a lot of sweet edible flesh on the fruit, but being the first fruit we harvest, tastes very good when I have been without fresh fruit for a few months. The loquat generally produces an abundant crop of fruit, but a severe winter freeze can kill the fruit. The tree itself seems to be able to take freezing weather quite well though. Some plums bloom early too, and are generally the second fruit to harvest. Peaches ripen in mid-summer, pears ripen around August, and citrus fruit around the end of the year. If you have a good orchard, you can have fresh ripe fruit for a lot of the year. Many fruits keep well for weeks, and most can be dehydrated to keep for months.

Dewberries are early berry producers, and are vine fruit that grow wild just about everywhere around here. Dewberries have a strong flavor and are very tasty, but the vines are thorny. The fruit, however, is well worth the danger. Dewberries are similar to raspberries and blackberries, and are such a dark purple color they look black when ripe. When dewberries bloom, the small white flowers first produce a green berry, which then turns red as it ripens, and finally black when the berry is mature. Dewberries grow much better in the heat of the south where I live, than do raspberries and blackberries. You really have to watch for snakes though when picking this fruit, as snakes can hide under the vines and bite you while you pick the fruit, which grows close to the ground. It is also a good idea to spray an insect repellent on your body and/or clothes to protect you from ticks, mosquitos and other tiny nasty critters, like chiggers, while picking dewberries. I like to freeze dewberries whole and dry on a metal tray or pan, and then store the frozen berries in re-sealable plastic bags. This makes them quite convenient to use, as they can be scooped out of the bag like marbles.

The dewberry is one of my favorites as they make excellent cobblers or pies, but what I like best about them, is they make a great "purple cow", which is a couple hands full of berries partially mashed in a glass with some sugar, with milk poured over and stirred good to dissolve the sugar. Very tasty! I freeze some berries every year and keep them in the freezer for times when I feel the need for purple, purple cow that is, long after the berry season has come and gone.

    I can tell you over and over, you must try to learn all you can throughout your life, and you will not likely listen to me. Just telling someone they need to do something, will not necessarily result in them taking your advice, and actually making learning a part of their life as they really should. I can tell you this though; eventually you will know I was right, and that you should have started the learning process a little earlier in your life. I am stressing you must take the offensive, and always stay in the learning mode, because the fact is, I cannot tell you everything you need to learn during your life, and I cannot make you smart. If you finish this book, you will be smarter than you are now, but you probably won't gain enough information by just reading this book to actually be a smart person. If you do not start the learning process right now, then I promise you, one day you will know I was right. Bank on it.

Chapter 3
College, Reading and Mental Strength

I will never claim to be the smartest person on planet Earth. There are many smart people on this planet, and considering how much I know about so many things, I think I am one of them, but I'm not THE smartest, not by a long shot. I am, however, certainly smart enough to help those at whom this book is aimed, the bottom 50% of the people on this planet, learn to be a little smarter than they were before they read this book. But more importantly, I hope to spark their interest to learn even more, so they can climb out of the bottom half and into the smarter half. There are now seven billion people on Earth. I'm betting half are not all that smart, and you are in the bottom half. Want to climb up to the top half?

Anyone can learn things from books. All you need to do is grab a book and start reading. And I'm not talking about reading fiction or a romance novel; I'm talking about non-fiction books and textbooks. Not as fun to read, but these books will give you more knowledge and help you become smarter. But I'm not trying to give you just book knowledge you can get easily on your own. I want to help you with the things I learned by working and doing things as a commercial fisherman, where I was very close to nature and all the wonderful things most people never get the chance to see up close, and later working as a contractor. I got the chance to learn about so many things most people never get the chance to learn. I used some of our natural resources to feed and support my family, but also learned about many creatures with no commercial value.

I attended college for four years, and got my Associate's Degree at two years. I attended college for two more years in pursuit of my Bachelor's Degree (B.S.), and majored in math with minors in chemistry, biology and history, but quit before getting my Bachelor's Degree because I was no longer learning anything. I was drinking too much and partying too much, and though I really should have devoted more time to my studies, I did not do it. I got married, which really cut down on the drinking and partying, but I could not focus on school. It was time to quit. For me, that was the right thing to do, but I hope you can learn from my mistake and push forward to achieve what I did not. If you are still in school, I urge you to not do what I did. Study a little harder and try to get your degree, but I cannot fault you if you do not, as I did not finish myself. At times I regret not getting my degree, but that is water under the bridge now, and I will never get my B.S. If you have the fortitude to get your degree though, do your best to do so.

After school, the rest of my life was mostly spent learning by doing. I did not study much at all while I was a commercial fisherman, but when I began my contracting career, I did study quite a bit. I studied manuals, brochures, and application guides, which were really quite boring, but necessary to learn the skills I needed as a contractor. Just because you are out of school, doesn't mean studying is over forever. There is always something that needs to be learned, and sometimes you need to do a lot of reading to gain the necessary information to be able to do the work well. In my case, this was the correct application of the protective coatings for commercial roofing, paving and masonry which would become a major portion of my livelihood. To better sell the coatings, I needed to know more about the products I was selling. I learned this by reading many brochures and product data bulletins, supplied by the manufacturer of the coatings. And I needed to learn more and better techniques about how to sell the coatings. This was accomplished by reading a lengthy sales manual produced by the manufacturer, and through several sales seminars offered by the manufacturer. So you see, there is always something to be learned, and some of this learning requires reading. Like it or not, that is the way it is, and it is quite boring at times, but very necessary. You may as well learn this now, and be prepared to do what is necessary to get the job done.

I did not read much for pleasure anymore, but when there was the rare occasion I did read something just for pleasure, I have enjoyed reading. But reading really was not what I enjoyed most. Now, at age 63, my eyes aren't that good anymore, and I don't wear eyeglasses, though I do have glasses to wear to see better when I need to see better, and I wear sunglasses most of the time while I am outside. If the book print is small, reading just seems to be a bother and my eyes seem to tire easily. Not really a good excuse though. There was one occasion when I decided I wanted to read something just for pleasure. That major reading accomplishment was finally reading a book I have wanted to read my entire life. I finally read *War and Peace*. Not light reading, and it was difficult, but I did get through it, and it was very enjoyable and satisfying. If you are up to the challenge, I challenge you to read it too. There are a couple things which made *War and Peace* really hard to read, and the first was there were so many characters. Their lives were so intertwined, that at times it was difficult to remember who was related to whom. It was so long, you learn a character, and then the character would disappear, and it may be awhile before the character resurfaces in the book. Then you get to wondering who the character is, and you can't remember who he or she is related to. The descriptions in the book were very lengthy and vivid, and I really got a feel for what was happening. I felt like I was there interacting with the characters, and could feel their pain and agony right along with them; so much so I even had some nightmares about the war. It was also a pretty good history lesson. It took months to finish, but was a good read and I am very glad I took on the project. I do highly recommend the book if you are up for the challenge, and I assure you it will be a challenge, but if you can get through it, you will have accomplished a great reading feat in your life.

Accomplish one great feat, and you will be ready for another. Maybe I'll read another great book when I finish writing mine. Life is about challenges, some of which you will take on because you want to take them on, and others of which you will have no choice. These challenges make life tough, but surviving a big challenge can make you feel much better about yourself, and your capabilities. All through life you will be given challenges, and you must take on these trials. You will always have setbacks, as I did with advanced calculus in college, but you must always try your best, but also be prepared to deal with those challenges that get the best of you. Always prepare to succeed all the time, and have the intestinal fortitude to succeed, but don't beat yourself up over a setback. Setbacks are a part of living and learning. You only fail when you stop trying.

Setbacks occur throughout life, and are a part of life, and you certainly had better know this. Life is never a bed of roses, and I don't care who you are, there will be many challenges in life, and some may be insurmountable. That is why I had a midlife crisis, and became a contractor after my commercial fishing business. Life is tough, and what doesn't kill you will make you stronger. You had better learn to be mentally strong and learn to cope with all the setbacks, both large and small, you will encounter throughout your life. I cannot teach you this. You just have to learn this on your own. And drugs and/or alcohol will not make you mentally strong, or solve your problems. If you have to turn to drugs or alcohol, this is a sign you are not mentally strong enough, and you had better find another way to deal with your problems, because drugs or alcohol will not help. You have to be optimistic, and dig way down into your gut, and find the strength to pull yourself up and move on. Tell yourself this obstacle will not get the best of you. Do whatever you need to do to move on, whether over or around your obstacle, but continue forward, always. Again, I cannot teach you this. Try to not let any obstacle get the best of you, but if you cannot get over the obstacle, there are ways around the obstruction. You just need to find a different path. I had to give up my commercial fishing career to pay my bills and feed my family. I chose a new path, and moved forward. That is what I did when I became a contractor. Whatever happens though, never give up on life, because there will always be obstacles, some small and some maybe quite large, but giving up on life cannot be an option.

Chapter 4
Language and Succeeding

I was never one to use a lot of foul language, but from time to time I will use it in life and in this book to emphasize something or other. It seems these days no one will listen to you, unless you swear a little or drop an F bomb here and there. I feel strongly about a lot of things, and you will know it when I do, but I will symbolize the F bomb in this book. I don't want you to get the idea I talk like this all the time, as I don't. Those of you in the ghetto, or wherever you might be, who talk with a trashy mouth all the time, are unemployed and have no friends other than your trash talking buddies, are not trying to improve and not trying to get a job, and have no interest in doing so, I have no time or sympathy for you. If the only real skill you have is stealing, and if you want to be the scum of the planet, that is your choice, and I hope you get everything you deserve, be it prison, death, or worse, a miserable life at a minimum wage dead end job, and no fun in life and no hope for the future. If you do not care about your life or your future, I do not care either.

If you are a trash talking bum, I want you to think, if that is at all possible, for a second, that you are an employer interviewing yourself for a job. Look at yourself and the way you dress and talk. Would you hire yourself for a management position? If you are looking for a job and are not dressed for, or act like you want the position, then you will not get the job and I have no pity for you at all. If your goal is to be a bum, then go ahead and do whatever you want, but I don't think I have ever heard anyone say they wanted to grow up to be a bum. They usually wanted to have some type of prestigious job, but never a bum. Do you want to be a bum? If so, then let it be, this book will not help you. If, on the other hand, you want to improve and make something out of yourself, then you need to get your act together and pay attention. I am handing you some important information which will help get you onto a path for a better life, but very little else will be given to you. You will need to learn, prepare and take what life has to offer. That is your job, and you will not succeed in life unless you put forth the effort, and the effort will need to be great. Even if you have a job, but are not advancing with the company, maybe it's your mouth and looks that are holding you back. Maybe you need to put forth a little more effort in this area.

You have the opportunity to be whatever you want in life. You have the opportunity to have enough money for yourself and your family. You have the opportunity to be happy and to have fun. You have the opportunity to be liked and respected, but while this is true, you also have the opportunity to go to prison, to be killed on the streets, and to live a miserable poor life with no hope, no way out and an early death. This is your choice, and you have the opportunity, no matter what shape your life is in currently, to turn your life around and make a future for yourself. Do you want to wallow around in the bottom of the barrel with the rest of your scummy buddies, or do you want to get out and make a decent life for yourself? The choice is always yours. You only have to decide to make the choice for a better life.

Whatever you decide is perfectly fine with me, and frankly I do not care what choice you make. If you make the wrong choice, then I hope you will be killed in the street by one of your scummy so called buddies. If you decide to make the right choice, then I wish you the best, because you will really have an uphill battle ahead of you. You will be challenged again and again, as you climb out of that nasty barrel. It will not be easy and you may get a little frustrated at times, but you must never give up and you must never quit. If you quit anywhere along the way, it will be a very quick and very nasty fall back to the bottom of the barrel.

If you should happen to make it out of the barrel, I assure you, you will be a much happier person and wish you had started the climb much sooner than you did. It will not be an easy climb, and you may even backslide a bit from time to time, and your success will not happen overnight. In fact, it may take years for you to reach a level of success you are happy with, but persistence and perseverance are always rewarded. It's your choice, and it's your life. You make the choice. Do it now.

Chapter 5
Around the Ranch
(The Early Years)

After I got out of college, I began my commercial fishing career. I learned a lot working for myself, and this would be a good place to start your education about my life and some pretty interesting things you will not likely learn anywhere else. But first, there are some interesting stories about my early years, as basically a wild child, running wild in the pastures around the house with my first cousin Steve. I would like to share these stories with you. While wild in most senses of the word, I was given a strong sense of right and wrong by my parents, so I was wild, but not mischievous.

Cousin Steve and I were the same age, two months apart, and were like brothers. I had no brothers, only two sisters, one of which I literally fought with my entire life. Steve had one sister and no brothers. Steve and I were best friends for many years, and were inseparable much of the time. We were always barefoot when it wasn't too cold. We ran around in the pasture barefoot, and ran into a few sticker burs from time to time, and they usually slowed me down a bit, but they didn't bother Steve so much. His feet were always a little tougher than mine. We usually carried guns, usually a shotgun when we got a little older, but a bb or pellet gun before we got old enough to carry a shotgun. We were always hunting something, and trampled all over snakes and never once got bit. That was just lucky, and both of us are really lucky to be alive today.

I remember once we were walking down a dirt road, two dirt paths where the car tires made trails, and were hunting dove. We had our shotguns ready and our eyes to the sky for the fast flying mourning dove. Suddenly, we heard a rattlesnake rattling its rattler on its tail, and we both stopped dead in our tracks and looked around. The rattlesnake was coiled up in Steve's path. He had walked right over the snake without stepping on it. The snake's life ended right then and there. We didn't eat the snakes we killed, but they made unique hatbands. We learned early in life how to skin the snakes and tan their hides.

Another time, we were duck hunting in the marsh, and about mid-morning, we heard one of Steve's dogs barking relentlessly. We went over to check out what she was barking at, and found a rattlesnake coiled up under a shrub. Being the kids we were, we saw the opportunity to claim another snake for a hatband. We were squatted down by the shrub with our shotguns, trying to find the best angle to shoot the snake, without messing up the snake, and thus ruining a good hatband. Steve came around to where I was squatting, and I got up to move farther to my left. When I did, Steve almost stepped on another rattlesnake stretched out where I was squatting. He got that hatband, and I got the one under the shrub. Another close call!

I think I was around eight years old, when I shot a shotgun for the first time. There was some shooting going on at the back of the house, and after much pestering, my dad finally let me shoot the gun. It was a single barrel 16-gauge shotgun, and was pretty heavy for a little guy like myself. I did get the gun to my shoulder, aimed and pulled the trigger. I think I hit what I was shooting at, but an instant after pulling the trigger, I was flat on my butt. The gun had no recoil pad, a pretty good kick to it and bruised my arm from the recoil. That wasn't something I would soon forget. I didn't ask to shoot the gun again, and didn't shoot another shotgun for several years. I stuck to my bb gun, which had no recoil.

When I did get a little older though, a shotgun was my gun of choice to carry and hunt with. We hunted geese and ducks in the fall, and always killed about as many as anyone else. In fact, Steve and I became very good hunters. Our dads would throw empty beer cans in the air for us to shoot. They couldn't throw them very well most of the time, especially after a few beers, and we never knew which direction the cans were going to go, but most of the time Steve and I managed to hit the cans. We didn't always hit the dove we hunted, as they were pretty fast flying birds, but as we grew older we didn't miss quite so much. Shotgun shells seemed to get more expensive from year to year, and we always tried to bring in enough game to pay for the ammo we used. I think for the most part, we did a pretty good job.

The single most important reason why we do not live under a dictatorship, or insanely brutal government in the US, is we as citizens own guns. We don't just own a few guns, we own a lot of guns and we know how to use them. Well, some of us know how to use them. What about you? Do you own a gun and know how to use it? If not, you should. I was raised with a gun in my hands. You have to be able to defend yourself against mayhem, and a gun puts you on an equal footing with those who would harm you. I can cut you in half at point blank range, or take you out half a mile away. I'm ready, are you? You are defenseless without a gun and also missing out on some fine game.

I guess you know by now, we had a ranch. Steve lived on one end of the ranch in an old brick house previously owned by Uncle Ernest on my dad's side. We originally lived in a wood frame house, until I was about five. My dad then built a brick home about a hundred yards from the wood frame home, on the opposite end of the ranch from where Steve lived. The home was mostly pink brick, which I think my mother liked, but I never cared much for the color. My room was blue, of course, so the color of the house didn't matter so much. My mother had a rose garden, and grew carnations in the big planter in front of the house. We had a big yard in front and back, as the house was built on an acre of land. Though we had a big yard, there was not much to hunt, and except for when the weather was very cold or really nasty, I tended to stray into the bigger pasture behind the house, which contained all the game I wanted or needed to hunt.

I only remember one story from the wood frame home

where we lived. There were several horses that roamed the pasture behind the house. They were not wild, but not gentle enough for kids to ride. My older sister and a cousin wanted to ride the horses one day when the horses came to the rear of the house, but they had no saddle or bridle. To test the horses, to see if they were gentle enough for my sister and cousin to ride, they used me as a guinea pig. They lured the horses in close with some feed, and put me on top of one horse. The horses did not appear to be wild, but started to walk away. The one I was on walked under a tree limb, which hit me, thus knocking me off the horse. I was not seriously injured as I landed on my head (I was very hard headed at that age), but had several abrasions from the tree limb and the fall to the ground. My sister told my mother I fell off the front porch. The front porch was only two feet high, and there was grass all around. My mother didn't believe their story for a second, and eventually got the truth out of the two gals. They got a well-deserved spanking. I remember the house was painted white, and there was a big live oak tree in the front yard, but that is about all I remember about this place.

I don't remember exactly how old I was, but we were living in the pink brick home. One night I had a nightmare, got tangled up in my bed clothes, jumped out of bed and took a bite out of the window sill. I busted my lip open and ripped out one of my permanent eye teeth. I remember being on my hands and knees on the floor with a big puddle of blood below my head. I don't remember crying, but am sure I did. Probably more like screaming than crying, but whatever, I attracted the attention of everyone in the house in the middle of the night. I had a big gap in my upper row of teeth, but the teeth later grew together. As a result, my upper row of teeth is very straight and you cannot tell I'm missing a tooth. Just one of those little stories you can never seem to forget. You probably have a few stories of your own, similar to mine. It is as though there is a force, telling us man is destined to a life of pain. We enter this world crying from day one, when we exit the womb. Maybe our life is nothing more than a test of strength, and we shall be tested repeatedly. Many of you may say God is that force. BS!

Living around cattle, there were blackbirds, grackles, cowbirds, and redwing blackbirds, which were always plentiful and made good targets for Steve and I to hone our hunting skills. My dad told me to not bother dove nests when they were laying eggs in the spring. Dove made their nests in trees, and their eggs are white. We didn't mess with them. We really liked to hunt the mourning dove, so we didn't do anything to interfere with their breeding. We were taught to protect the future of the game we hunted. Of course, we were always after jackdaw (aka grackle) eggs. The only problem with hunting jackdaw eggs was they made their nests high in the tree tops. They were very hard to get at, as the limbs were very limber way up at the top of the trees, but Steve and I managed to get quite a few every year. We broke them, usually in egg fights, because there were always too many grackles. Grackle eggs are a shade of turquoise with tiny black speckles. We learned to climb trees very well, and I don't recall Steve or me ever falling out of a tree. Most of the bird nests were in mesquite trees, and they are thorny. We did get a thorn from time to time, but nothing serious. Regardless of what we were doing, we were always learning. There was a lesson or two in everything we did.

Speaking of tree climbing, Steve and I spent a lot of time in the trees of Monkey Mott next to his house. Mustang grapes as we called them, a type of muscadine grape, grew wild in those trees, as well as other places. Steve and I spent a lot of time in those trees eating the grapes. They were strong flavored and sweet, but tart too, and would bite your tongue a bit when you ate them. We also smoked the vines. We would break off little dead twigs about the size of a cigarette, and light and smoke them. We learned to smoke very early, as our parents smoked cigarettes, and when we couldn't find a smoke anywhere else, we smoked small limbs of the mustang grape. Our grape vine smokes also bit our tongues. Our parents would hide their cigarettes from us, so we seldom got real cigarettes, so we had to improvise. We made corn cob pipes, and at times we smoked some really nasty stuff, like shredded hickory we found one time on a vacation trip to Garner State Park. It was used for starting campfires, and we tried to smoke it in our corn cob pipes. Often we would find cigarette butts or cigar butts, and get the tobacco out of those. They made a pretty good smoke, compared to the grapevines or some of the other shit we smoked.

Garner State Park was a regular vacation spot, west of San Antonio, for the family. Steve would often go with us. We would basically do the same things there as we did at home, but these trips were really special for us. The river at home was always muddy and murky, and the creek was nearly dry and stagnant most of the time. The only time we had clear water to swim in, was when we went to a pool somewhere. The water at Garner State Park was a naturally clear mountain stream. We spent most of our time swimming, and could see fish swimming, usually near the bottom. As there was no hunting, we spent a lot of time fishing. We were in our swim trunks 24 hours a day, and caught enough perch, the only fish we could catch in abundance, to have a meal on these small but tasty fish.

There was a small cave in one of the mountains at the park called "Old Baldy". Baldy was a bare (no trees) round top mountain at the edge of the park. There was a rocky trail leading up to this cave, that was not too steep, but the trail was very rocky, which made the climb difficult, as you would continually slide back downhill, but eventually we made the trip to the cave. There were katydids in the cave, which are similar to crickets. We used the katydids for bait to catch our fish. The katydids were difficult to keep in our pockets, as we kept them alive, and they didn't want to stay in our pockets. We usually managed to make it down from the mountain with enough to fish with. These little weekend vacations always seemed to go by a little too fast, and before we knew it, we were back home.

There were a few quail on our ranch, but we didn't bother them much. They were pretty rare, and we didn't want them to become extinct. Probably something our dads told us. The quail had a tough time increasing their population, because they spent most of their time on the ground, and they made their nests on the ground, which made them easy targets for predators. We had foxes, one such predator, on the ranch, though seeing them was rare. In all my life, I have only seen two foxes on the place. We also had jack rabbits and cottontail rabbits. We didn't mess with the jack rabbits much, but the cottontail rabbit made a really tasty meal. My dad would let the owner of the local restaurant hunt the jack rabbits, and he would use them for the meat in the chili at the restaurant. The meat of the jack rabbit is a little tough, but makes very good chili.

Next to our ranch was a huge marsh of the Guadalupe River delta, and Steve and I spent a lot of time in that marsh. We were trespassing, but no one was going to catch us, and no one tried. We were the only ones who ever went into the marsh. We tramped around in the salt grass, a clump grass with needle-like, round leaves, much like pine needles only longer, pointy and sharp. The clumps grew up to about two feet high, and made a soft place to sit and rest, if you pushed the needles over so they didn't stick you.

We tramped around in the mud and muck in search of wild duck. There were always plenty of the smaller teal, green wing mostly with a few green feathers on each wing, but some red wing teal too. Once I killed a cinnamon teal, which was the only one I ever killed. This must have been a fairly rare bird. It was a very pretty bird with cinnamon reddish brown colors. We also killed widgeon, goldeneye, gadwall, pintail and plenty of spoonbills (aka smiling mallards). Mallard ducks were the real prizes we hunted, as they were larger and premium quality ducks. They seemed to taste better than the other species of duck. The hen, or female, was a mottled brown, black and tan with orange feet and bill. The drake, or male, was grayish and had a green head and curled up tail feathers. We didn't kill many mallards, but felt very lucky when we did. They were premium ducks, and we considered them trophies. The smiling mallards were a different type of duck, but looked a lot like the mallard hen, only smaller with a longer flattened bill, which made it look like it was always smiling, hence the name smiling mallard. These ducks tasted a little muddy when cooked and eaten, so we tried to avoid killing them, but when ducks were scarce, we took whatever came our way. The muddy taste was due to this particular duck's diet. The flattened bill is ideal for straining mud for food living in the mud. Apparently, the duck swallowed a significant amount of mud too, therefore, the muddy taste of the duck. All the time we spent in the marsh, we knew very well the taste of the mud there.

    The black duck, also called a black mallard, was plentiful, and we usually killed two or three a season. They were good ducks, and both the male and female look like a mallard hen, only a little darker in color. The black duck is a native of the south, and is the only duck which does not migrate north in the spring. It stays here and rears its young in the heat of summer. The wood duck is probably the most beautiful duck, with a lot of bright colors. I think I only killed one or two of these in all my years hunting. I later avoided killing them because of their beautiful colors.

    We mostly ate what we killed. We would kill just about anything, when we went on camping trips in different areas of the pasture. We ate just about anything too, so we knew what tasted good and what didn't. Robin redbreast tastes pretty good, but not much meat. Among some of the foul tasting critters were blackbirds and nutria, which was nothing but a giant rat, nearly the size of a raccoon. Raccoon is mighty greasy. Meadowlarks didn't taste very good either. Squirrels are excellent, as are cottontail rabbits.

    There were always a lot of geese every year. Our property bordered the marsh, and there was a bluff separating the high land. We hunted along this bluff, as the geese spent their nights in the marsh, and in the mornings, these geese would fly toward the bluff, as they made their way to the corn fields and rice fields. The geese would fly up from the marsh and attain a certain height, as they flew out of the marsh. When they reached the headland, however, suddenly they were — feet lower, because they didn't see the rise until they were at the bluff, and hadn't increased their distance from the ground. The bluff was about sixty feet high with respect to the marsh. When the geese reached the bluff, and they never seemed to remember the cliff was there, they were well within range of our guns. This bluff was always hunted when goose season was open, and we wanted geese to eat. When most people were having turkey for Thanksgiving, while we sometimes had turkey too, we always had goose and dressing.

Literally millions of geese made residency in this marsh every winter. They were mostly Canada geese, snow geese, blue geese, with a few speckled belly geese. The Canada goose is a grey goose with a black neck and a white band under its head. The Canada goose has two varieties, the greater and the lesser. The basic difference was size, the lesser being smaller. Snow geese were of course white, with a little black on the wing tips. The smaller Ross's goose was also white, but with no black on the wing tips. The speckled belly or bar breast, correctly known as the white fronted goose, was pretty rare and quite a trophy. The speckled belly has a gray breast with black bars, and makes a cackling sound, which is distinguishable from the other geese (if you know your geese that is). The black bars make its breast look speckled with black spots when flying overhead. Due to a government breeding program, the speckled belly is fairly common these days. We didn't concern ourselves so much about the correct names of many animals. We had our own names and we always knew what we were talking about. I guess we came up with our own names for some things, due to being young and misunderstanding what our relatives was telling us. This probably makes for a lot of misinformation in the world today.

We mostly hunted the Canada goose and the speckle belly, and these two species were the best geese to eat and the easiest to clean, as long as we killed the older geese and not the yearlings. The yearlings always had a lot of pin feathers (immature feathers), and they were more difficult to pick due to these pin feathers. It was pretty difficult to tell the older geese from the younger geese at times, but Steve and I got pretty good at picking out the mature geese. The lead goose in a group was always a mature goose. I had relatives from Oklahoma who would come down every winter to hunt geese, and we always killed a lot of them and ate very well. Food was never a problem around our place. We hunted, and always had beef cattle, and mama raised chickens. We had a milk cow, so we always had milk, butter, eggs, and fresh meat. Mama also had a vegetable garden, and we always had fresh veggies, though I didn't like many of them. I was a meat and potatoes guy. Mama said I would eat okra when I was young, but I don't remember this. I must have been pretty young. I guess mom and dad worked really hard to provide food for us, and I did a fair share of providing my own food too.

One thing my dad made was stink cheese. I don't really know how he made it, but mama would not let him make it in the house. It was a soft cheese, made out of cow milk, and was just barely thick enough to spread with a knife. Was better dipped and spread with a spoon. One thing I do know was daddy kept it in the garage, and it really stunk. I would see the cheese in a dish in the garage, and it was just sitting there bubbling. This was the nastiest, supposedly edible stuff, I have ever smelled. Yuk! Everyone has different tastes, and what may be candy to one, may be inedible to another. It can be fun exploring new foods and tastes. I know I eat more foods now, than I ate ten years ago, and this was through experimentation. Try something new, you might learn you like it. I do not, however, recommend stink cheese.

It is time for a test, to see if you are remembering what I am trying to teach you. This test is for you to test your reading skills. There will be no grade, unless you give yourself one. I will tell you where you can find the answer to the questions, but I hope you don't need to look.

What type of fruit is a loquat?

1. Peach
2. Pear
3. Plum

Answer on page 19

What product did I sell when I started my contracting business?

1. Paints
2. Coatings
3. Oil

Answer on page 23

Do you need to concentrate a little more? If you are not remembering what you are reading, then reading is not helping you. Maybe you need to read a little slower, and pay more attention to what you are reading. I don't think my story is that boring is it? There will be more tests later.

Chapter 6
More Around the Ranch

A creek ran through our property, and Cousin Steve and I spent a lot of time around, and in this creek. We fished for perch mostly, as it wasn't a very large creek, except when we had a major flood, when it could swell to a hundred yards or more across. Occasionally, we would get lucky and catch a catfish, but mostly just perch. There were also plenty of snakes along the creek, and sometimes we would catch one or two with a loop at the end of a piece of string, and hang them in a tree by the string to die. They would always go after our perch on a stringer, and we would use the perch to attract them through the string snare. They were mostly moccasins, and were extremely poisonous. Catching these snakes may seem a little dangerous, but not as dangerous as leaving them alone and letting one sneak up on us, and maybe getting bitten by one of these dangerous snakes.

I am telling you stories like this, because when and if you get out into nature, doing whatever you might be doing, whether camping, hiking, fishing or whatever, you really need to be aware of the critters that may also be around you. Your life can very well depend on your knowledge of the animals out there with you, and your keen eyes in spotting these animals, before they get you. This is true in all areas of your life. Learn more about your surroundings, and keep your eyes wide open at all times, and be aware of the dangers that exist. At times though, your safety may depend upon your dumb luck too, but you cannot always depend upon just luck. You may be lucky at times, but keeping your eyes open will greatly increase your chances of keeping out of harm's way. The same can also be true when in the city, and keeping your eyes open for the most dangerous animals around, the human animals, which can and will harm you.

There were a few wild plum thickets along our creek at high water level, and Steve and I would check the thickets for plums every spring. My grandmother on my dad's side also lived at one edge of the ranch, not very far from where I lived. She had a tangerine tree which produced the sweetest fruit. There were mulberry trees, pecan trees, pomegranate bushes and lots more. We would fish for crawdads and crabs in the creek, and though it would take half a day or more sometimes to get a meal, we were persistent and patient. Sometimes it took a little ingenuity to find and harvest the meal. Are you getting the idea about much of our diet? Steve and I were always hunting something, and our moms seldom had any idea where we were during the day, or what we were doing. We seldom got hungry, because there was always something around to eat. We even ate the seeds from a little bull nettle plant, which grew about a foot high, and had tiny needles all over it. It produced a seed about the size of a marble, covered with needles too. There were usually three or four nuts inside very hard shells, covered with a very hard peel. This was a tough snack to get at, but what the hell, we were kids.

Our land bordered on the Guadalupe River, which was across the marsh from the pasture where we spent most of our time. We also had another separate plot of land farther down the river, toward the bay into which the river dumped. This plot of land, closer to the bay, was a better place to fish. Steve and I spent a lot of time there too. We had to drive around through town to get there, as it was a really tough walk through the marsh, and quite a distance away. We didn't have a driver's license, but we drove anyway. We learned to drive very young, first driving on the ranch, and then later when we proved we could drive well enough, on the streets and highways. We caught catfish, and in the winter time we also caught redfish, or red drum, that would come into the lower end of the river when the weather got really cold; below freezing. The shallow bay would cool off quickly when the weather turned cold, and the redfish would come into the warmer water in the river, which was much deeper and didn't cool off like the bay did. It does not get below freezing much around here, but sometimes it gets really cold; down into the teens occasionally, not really so cold by some standards, but plenty cold for us southerners. Cousin Steve and I would get plenty cold swimming, chasing downed ducks, and fishing in the winter time. We were always wet and muddy, but we always brought game in to eat. We never let a little water, mud or numbness in the hands and feet keep us from the game we hunted. What didn't kill us made us tougher, and nothing killed us, though critters and nature tried.

As we lived on a ranch, there was always ranch work to do. When we got old enough to do the real ranch work, Steve and I were always in the thick of it. Our dads made certain of that. I remember one instance during the winter time, when it was not all that cold, but cold nevertheless, some fencing needed fixing across the creek running through the property. We were the kids, so we went into the water to string the barbed wire, while our dads gave us instructions from the dry creek bank. We strung the wire, while an alligator about six feet long swam nearby, watching our every move. He was not going to bother us, and we were not afraid of it either. There was not much Steve and I was afraid of. We grew up strong and tough, fending for ourselves, and never looked back, except when we heard the rattlesnake we had just trampled over rattling its tail. That was bad news for the snake.

Steve and I would go on camping trips in the pasture as we got a little older, and we really liked camping. Sometimes we would take a friend or a cousin, and sometimes ride our horses, or at times just head out on foot. We would not take any food and we ate what we killed. This would set the stage for later camping trips with my son, nephew, brother-in-law, or son-in-law. We eventually got to where we would take a few potatoes and some butter, salt and bait for our fishing rods. We would take our rod and reels and guns, and we seldom went hungry. In fact, there was a time or two, where I had to go home to get an ice chest and ice, to keep some of the game we caught and killed.

One camping trip, a cousin was along on his horse, and Steve and me on our horses. This cousin was a big fella and had a big horse, Big John, and the name suited him well. We took some extra gear on this particular trip, and the biggest horse of course carried the extra gear. There were some pots and pans hung on Big John's saddle, and no sooner than we got started, the pots and pans began to clang together. Big John didn't like this noise and began to buck. Bucking only made the clanging worse. This was quite a show. I think this was the only trip we took more than one pot or pan. Another lesson learned.

Camping teaches a lot of skills, and we learned these skills very well. We learned to build a fire and clean game to cook over an open campfire. We ate very well, and on some very tasty wild game much of the time, but there were also times when game was scarce, and we learned what not to eat by experience. We learned to get around in the dark, and to build a small makeshift tent to sleep in, or a hammock to sleep on. We never had a real tent when we were younger, but eventually acquired this luxury item. Everything we had was makeshift in the early years. Sometimes we just slept under the stars. We learned to protect ourselves from not just the very large animals in the wild, but the very small critters which were more common, and usually the biggest pests.

There is one thing I have never told anyone, until now. Steve and I were hunting one day, and a cottontail rabbit jumped out in front of me and ran to my left. Steve was also back and to my left, and I knew exactly where he was when I swung my shotgun around to the left to shoot the rabbit. But what I did not expect was for Steve to run up between me and the rabbit. He also pointed his shotgun at the rabbit, and my gun was pointed dead center of Steve's back, and my finger on the trigger. I was ready to shoot, and I can still feel how much pressure I had on the trigger, and it was enough for the gun to shoot, or very close to it. The thought ran through my mind that I had shot and killed my cousin, but the gun didn't go off as I eased my finger off the trigger and raised my gun. I don't know why the gun didn't go off because I still believe I had enough pressure on the trigger for the gun to shoot. The difference between Steve's life and death had to be infinitesimally small. I was so relieved it didn't go off, and have thought about this incident, from time to time, for 50 years. That could have really f_#%ed up my life. I'm glad it didn't. I'm sure Steve will be glad too, when he reads this book and finds this out. It REALLY would have f_#%ed up his life. I never told him.

Chapter 7
Still on the Ranch

My dad worked hard, with a regular job as a gauger for a local pipeline company in our county. When crude oil is pumped out of the ground into storage tanks, the amount of oil in the tanks must be measured. This is the job of a gauger. A metal tape measure with a weight on the bottom is used to measure the depth of, not just the amount of oil in the tank, but how much water is at the bottom of the tank, so an accurate measurement of the amount of just the oil in the tank can be calculated. There is usually a small amount of water in the oil pumped out of the ground. When pumped into the storage tanks, the water settles to the bottom of the tank. Oil is lighter than water. There is a white paste of some sort, smeared on the bottom of the tape, which would turn pink when it came into contact with the water in the bottom of the tank. This paste was not affected by the oil. The upper edge where the water turned the paste pink would indicate the bottom level of the oil in the tank. The upper level of the oil in the tank was indicated by the highest spot where the oil wet the tape, which was dry when inserted into the oil. The calculation of the volume of the oil is based on the depth of the oil and the size of the tank. The oil is pumped out of the tanks through pipelines to the refinery, and the tanks measured again, to calculate the amount of oil pumped out of the tanks. The tanks are then filled again, and the process repeated. This was my dad's regular job, and he did this job forty hours a week.

But this wasn't my dad's only job. He, along with my mother, also ran the local water company, owned a beer joint or at least the building it was in, which he later turned into a laundry mat, and owned the local drug store and fountain. With my uncle, Steve's dad, my dad also ran a ranch with over a hundred head of cattle. My uncle and dad were partners in the ranch, and co-owned the land and the cattle. They also drilled a couple oil wells on the property, which luckily at least paid for themselves, but didn't make any real money. My dad really worked hard to try to make a better life for us, and I think he was reasonably successful at this, though we were never rich. There had to be a lot of stress that went along with this chore, which is maybe why he drank on weekends. The drinking didn't solve anything though, and actually made things worse.

My mom worked equally hard raising chickens, taking care of and milking our jersey cow, making butter, doing a lot of cooking, running the water office, running the drug store, and also running the local telephone company switchboard, when phone service came to town. I don't know if they owned the phone company, but at least ran it. Mom worked hard at home raising three kids, but we mostly raised ourselves. We kept our rooms cleaned and helped around the house doing chores, to keep the household running smoothly. My mom also drank, but never to excess. I don't ever recall her being drunk, but my dad got there many times.

About the only thing I can actually remember learning from my dad, was to not kill mockingbirds, which by the way was the first bird I killed with my new bb gun. The mockingbird was the state bird I learned, and that one was the first and only one I ever killed. Yes, I did get into trouble for killing that one. Of course, I learned a lot more from my dad, but it was not because he was trying to teach me anything. I learned by watching what he did, and later did the same chores while he did other chores. I learned to build fence, repair washing machines and dryers in the laundry mat, and repair doors, floors, and windows and so many other things too numerous to name. I really did learn a lot from my dad by doing things together, whether or not he wanted me helping, but I probably didn't give him a choice at times.

One of the worst chores was working on fence. Barbed wire always cuts and sticks you sooner or later, even if you wear gloves, and these gloves had better be leather. Cotton gloves and barbed wire do not go together, and if you try it you will soon find out the cotton cloth will not stop or even slow down a barb. We always had to dig a post hole or two, and tamp in the post about eighteen inches into the ground. Posthole diggers will work you pretty good, and the holes always had to be a little deeper according to my dad, than I thought was necessary. But he was the one who knew how to do the job and I was the apprentice, so the holes were always dug to his specification. Later, we used treated round posts rather than cedar posts, which were much easier to drive a steeple into, but driving the post into the ground was the real chore. Steeples are used to hold the strands of wire in place on the posts. The treated posts were pointed with a chainsaw, and driven with a post driver. I think our post driver was homemade, as it was a six-inch pipe with a steel handle on each side, welded shut on one end. Doesn't sound so bad huh? Well, the driver weighed forty-eight pounds, and you place the driver over the top of the post and try to hammer it into hard dry ground a few times, and you will soon learn how quick your arms can turn to jelly from working the heavy weight of the driver. I still have this driver and have used it many times. It is not the chore it was when I was younger.

My mom was a great cook, and we couldn't wait for her to cook our favorite treat, chocolate fudge, which she made on a regular basis. At times she would get really busy with work, and not make any fudge. I think I was about ten years old, when I decided to take it upon myself to make the fudge. I overcooked the first batch, and then undercooked the second batch; we had to eat it with a spoon. It never set up, and the first batch was as hard as peanut brittle. I liked cooking, and these first batches of fudge were the beginning of my love for cooking.

I still like to cook to this day, and have made some original recipes the family really seems to like. One is dirty spaghetti, which is ground meat, onions, black olives, mushrooms, Ro-tel tomatoes and green chilies, cream of chicken and cream of mushroom soups, just about every spice I own, and of course, spaghetti. I'm sure I left out a few things, but these are the bulk of the ingredients. I basically threw in everything I liked, that would go with the ground meat. This is how I cook a lot of meals, and most are one skillet, or one pot dishes. Also, by the time all the ingredients are in and the meal is ready, there is usually enough left over for another meal, or two or three. Anyway, I like to cook, and I like to eat my own cooking, because I always cook to my tastes, not anyone else's. Others seem to like my cooking too.

What I remember about home life was it seemed to be nothing really special. We worked, went to school and played, and I don't remember much of any significance, except holidays. Christmas and Thanksgiving were always fun. We also had the occasional family get-together, mostly barbecues and beer parties. Other than that, I went to school and played outside and never saw my parents much. Christmas and the 4th of July were always more special, because of the fireworks we could buy during these times.

My dad was an alcoholic, and was a mean son-of-a-bitch when he was drunk, which is probably why I didn't spend much time around home, when I didn't have to study or eat a meal, especially on weekends. I don't think my dad was a bad father, as he always worked hard, trying new things and taking care of old things. He was a good provider. When he drank though, he turned into a Mr. Hyde, and was mean and not good to be around. My mother fought with him at times, but mostly just let him sleep it off.

I was always doing something constructive, and whatever I was doing, I was learning through making errors much of the time, but ultimately succeeding. Over the years, I got much better at whatever I was doing, and learned to do more and did it better. I guess most of what we learn is learned by doing things. When you are not eating, bathing, or sleeping, you need to be doing. It does not matter a whole lot what you are doing, as long as it is something constructive. Do something constructive and use your imagination to come up with new ideas, to create things which will make life better. In the early years, building a tree house, or growing something, building bird traps, or finding new sources of treats like pecans, plums, or new fishing holes were some of the constructive adventures which made life fun, and improved my situation over the previous day. Doing is the key to learning more. Study your surroundings and find ways to improve upon what you have. Learn what kinds of plants and animals are in your life. Do you have access to wildlife? What can you grow? What can you build? What do you need to do to make things happen? Just do it.

I guess my mom and dad really did teach me something, and that was if you can only do one thing, you are setting yourself up for failure. If you can do anything you put your mind to, through years of learning to do many different things, and learning to cope with change, then, you can always survive. I guess I could consider myself a "Jack of all trades". My mom and dad had many projects during their lives, and it didn't matter if one business venture failed, as they always had several irons in the fire. They always were working hard to put food on the table, paying their bills and even had some left over for vacations. They took chances with new ventures, and no matter what happened, they survived. I will survive too, no matter what happens. Are you set up for failure, or success?

It is not enough to just work hard though. You need space too. We always had plenty of room to run around. We had acres and acres of land, where we would not likely run into another living soul. Maybe we would run into a wild animal or two, but we always had plenty of wide open area around us. If you don't have space, maybe you need to rethink where you are living. Everyone needs room to expand their minds and grow their lives. If you don't have the space where you currently live, maybe you need to move to a place where you have a little more room. Of course, some people need more acreage than others. I happen to be one who needs a lot of space.

If you are living with your parents, moving may not be possible. A job might limit what you can do as far as creating your own space, if you are out on your own. But when you can, you need to find your space, and always work toward finding enough legroom to limit your interaction with others. Overcrowding always causes problems, and everyone has to have their space. Find yours.

I was a little on the shy side, and pretty much a bookworm, when I was in school. As a result, I was bullied in and out of school from time to time. I never talked to my parents about being bullied, and dealt with it on my own. I was never a good fighter, and got a bloody nose a time or two, but those things go away. You hear about someone committing suicide from being bullied these days, and yes suicide has crossed my mind a few times, but I never seriously considered suicide a possibility for me. There was just too much to live for. I always thought suicide had to hurt, no matter how you decided to do it, and I didn't like pain. What if I botched an attempt at suicide? That has to really hurt! I had enough pain in my life, with the tooth that was ripped out of my mouth when I took a bite out of a window sill, a boil I had cut out of my butt, sunburns, poison ivy, chiggers and the like. For me to add more pain on top of what I already had, didn't seem like a good option. It is hard for me to see how someone can get desperate enough to commit suicide. I think these people are weak minded and genetically inferior, and probably really need to die to protect the gene pool. If you have suicide on your mind, then go right ahead and do yourself in. You will get no pity from me, and you will add to the space we all desperately need. If you really are considering suicide, there *is* a good life out there for you somewhere, if you will search for it. Go find it, or die; your choice.

I grew up big and strong; it didn't seem to take that long. No one bullied me after I got out of high school. You bullies are a bunch of stupid morons who never made good grades in school, and I guess you had to make up for your own inferiority by bullying other people. After you grew up, you are probably some of the same stupid people who are f_#%ing up this country now. You probably really screwed up your life, and if you want to commit suicide, then please feel free to do so.

I remember when I got my first horse. He was black and a

real nag. I don't think dad paid much for the horse, but a horse is a horse when you are a kid. Steve and I were never taught how to ride a horse by our parents; we just got on and did it. I guess watching a few western movies on TV helped here. We learned to put on a bridle and saddle after being shown one time. Also, bridles and saddles broke over time, and we were not shown how to repair them, but we learned. If they didn't stay repaired, we soon learned to repair them better. You pick yourself up off the ground and chase down your horse a few times, and you'll learn to fix them better. Again, I was learning by doing, and learning to do things better by making mistakes.

Probably a big mistake was learning to ride horses bareback. You'll see why in a minute. I did this often and got pretty good at it. My cousin Steve had a couple black and tan hound dogs named Lucky and Happy. Turned out Lucky was not that lucky, as he did not live long. I don't remember how he died, but only that he did. We chased jack rabbits with the dogs, much like a fox and hound chase. Jack rabbits were large rabbits, but what made them noticeable were their very long ears. One day we were chasing jack rabbits with Happy, and I was riding my horse bareback. We were running along, and suddenly my horse decided to stop. There was nothing to hold me back, and I went flying over my horse's head. I flew over his head with my arms spread like a bird, and landed face first in the dirt. I guess my left arm hit first, as it popped the radius bone. It didn't hurt that much, but I could see it was bent just behind the wrist. I tried to straighten it, but when I pulled it straight, a sharp pain ran up my arm. That was a really bad idea and another lesson learned. There are two bones in the forearm, the radius and the ulna. Not enough knowledge to make you smart, but another tidbit of knowledge nevertheless. Learn enough little tidbits over the years, and you will be just a little bit smarter than the next guy.

I was taken to the doctor and he set my arm, after an injection with a very large needle numbed the wrist. I spent the next six weeks with a plaster of Paris cast on my left arm. As I am left handed, this made school work more difficult. I could not write with my left hand, so I learned to write a little with my right. I remember my left arm swelled, and I had to keep my arm above my heart much of the time for a few days, to keep the swelling down. And the cast began to make my arm itch after a while. Scratching the itch was difficult until the swelling went down a bit, then a butter knife did the trick.

Another thing I remember was my cousin's horse. His name was Booger Red, a spirited little red horse with a white star in the middle of his forehead. Steve didn't ride bareback as much as I did, because every time he went to get on Booger Red, he would tend to buck a little, until Steve rode some of the friskiness out of him. It was a little rodeo just about every time Steve and I went for a ride. I don't think Steve ever fell off, but he would surely have done so, had he not put the saddle on first. Steve was always good for a laugh when Booger Red went to bucking.

We worked cattle usually a couple times a year. This was a big event for Steve and me, and we learned to drive cattle into the pens across the creek. We started at one end of the property, with usually about seven or eight other cowboys, and drove the cattle across the creek in a shallow spot, and into the pens. Our horses didn't always want to cross the creek, and after a hundred plus cattle went across, it got pretty boggy. Cattle have split hooves, which helps them to not bog down in the mud so much. Horses have single hooves, and will tend to sink into the mud a bit more, and the horses didn't like this, and for good reason. They can break a leg fighting to get out of the mud. Of course, I don't think this ever happened on our ranch.

When we got the cattle into the pens, they were separated and the calves cut out by themselves. The cows were vaccinated with injections for leptospirosis, red water, and anthrax. Then we clipped the horns, if needed, to keep the cattle from hurting each other seriously when they fought, and from hurting us too, for that matter, when working them. When the horn tips are clipped, blood would squirt all over the place for a minute or two, until the blood coagulated and they sealed over. The cattle would then be sprayed for flies, lice, ticks, and skin irritations. The calves would be earmarked, vaccinated for blackleg, the bull calves castrated, and in the fall, the heifer calves to be kept for breed stock would be branded. The calves were worked one at a time, and were usually in a small area of the pens. They were roped one at a time and processed. Steve and I liked to rope and throw the calves, and got pretty good at it eventually. I say eventually, because at times some of the calves weighed almost as much as we did. As we grew older, this task became easier. When we worked the cattle in the fall, the older cows and bull calves would be taken to market and sold, and the heifers that would be kept for breed stock, would be kept in the pens and fed for a while to wean and gentle them down.

We were kids and stunk to high heaven when we were through, but we sure felt like men when we ate dinner with the rest of the cowboys at the local restaurant when all the work was finished. We had our boots on and cowboy hats with our snakeskin hatbands on them, and with cow shit, cattle spray, grass stains, blood and dirt all over us when we went to eat. We washed our hands and faces, but we still smelled pretty strong. Luckily, we couldn't smell ourselves or each other. We didn't care though, we were kids, but we were also COWBOYS!

Chapter 8
Rockport and Playing

Steve and I were seldom bored. We would always find something to do. If we were not fishing or swimming in the creek, climbing the trees in Monkey Mott, or hunting dove, geese or ducks, we would find a red ant bed and kill ants. We would find that perfect stick with a knot on the end, and sit around the bed for hours, killing ants one or two at a time. We were gods, wielding death and destruction without mercy. The ant beds were four or five feet in diameter, with trails leading to the center of the bed. The center of the beds would have no grass. The ants cleared the center area of all vegetation. We would kneel by one of the trails leading to the bed and slaughter the ants. We would usually eventually wipe out the bed. If we didn't wipe out all the ants, we would come back the next day and finish the job. We didn't get bitten much, but did occasionally. After a while, we learned to be a little more careful to watch for stray ants sneaking up behind us. There was always one or two, that would escape our eagle eyes and get us. I wish now, we had not killed so many of these red ants, as they are almost extinct around here. They were not eradicated by Steve and me, but by other predators, and especially fire ants, which have become a really big pest. I would much rather have the red ants than the fire ants.

Before Steve moved to the ranch, he lived in the nearby city of Rockport, with his mom and dad. Rockport was a seaport town, and I would visit him every chance I got. There was always plenty to do around town. This meant fishing and swimming most of the time, and we did plenty of both. We also caught blue crabs in the ski basin at the bay front. The ski basin was an enclosed saltwater area, with a little cut going out into the bay. The lagoon was dredged out to be deeper, so people could water ski around and around a central island.

Steve and I would ski there when we could get our dads to take us. We were not allowed to run the boat by ourselves. We were not old enough, so could only go skiing when they would take us. We did get to go regularly, and both Steve and I got pretty good and skied often on one ski. As Steve was a little smaller and lighter than I was, he could also ski barefoot. He would get up on two skis, then drop one, then the second ski. I was too heavy for this with the boat we had, which was not fast enough for me to ski barefoot.

The ski basin was only about four city blocks from Steve's house, and we spent plenty of time catching blue crabs in the shallow waters bordering the ski area. The water level was pretty consistent at about a foot deep in these shallows. We would walk around with our long handle dip nets, dragging a metal wash tub about two and a half feet in diameter, onto which we tied a short piece of rope. We walked around netting the crabs and putting them into the washtub. When we had enough for a meal, usually about a dozen, we went home and cleaned the crabs. Steve's mom would boil them up for us, and we would pig out on the delicious meat. When we got our fill, we would usually rest a while; then were off on another adventure.

Steve's dad's main job was working at the local carbon black plant. The plant was just outside of Rockport, and was always shrouded in a cloud of black smoke. My uncle picked up the nickname Smokey for working at this plant. Much of the time you could not see most of the plant, as the cloud of smoke was that thick. The nickname stuck until his death, though he quit working at the plant many years before he died.

Steve and I always wore our swimsuits and seldom wore a shirt. Sometimes we would get a little too much sun, but most of the time we tanned pretty well. If we wanted to go fishing, we seldom used a store bought rod and reel. We could usually scrounge up some twine and a hook or two and a stick for a pole. We never let the lack of things stop us from doing whatever we wanted to do. We would spend a lot of time around the boat harbor, and when a boat came in, we could usually talk them out of a little bait. Sometimes we would scrounge around to find and sell soda bottles to buy some bait, when all else failed. We would never say die though. We always came up with ways to get what we needed.

Rockport had a lot of festivals for the tourists, and there would also be games for the kids. This is where I learned to shoot a long bow. We would shoot the arrows at balloons to win prizes. There were also other games, but I don't remember them. Of course, there were cotton candy and candy apples, which were really rare treats for us kids. There were carnival rides, but we seldom had enough money to ride them. We couldn't spend what we didn't have. This would be a good lesson for our government to learn.

My dad and uncle liked to fish regularly, and it was a real treat when they would take Steve and me fishing or floundering. I remember getting my first store bought rod and reel, and my dad and uncle took us fishing in the boat, out in the bay, there at Rockport. I caught my first redfish, or red drum, out there. The redfish was a good eating fish that was also a pretty fish, with a black spot on each side of its tail, the only fish I know with this distinguishing characteristic. Occasionally, you will find a redfish which has more than one spot on each side of its tail, and sometimes as many as three or more. I later learned, while there are many good eating fish, catfish are the best to eat in my opinion. Most fish don't really seem to have much taste. Catfish have a fishy taste I really like, as long as they are not too big and the fishy taste gets exceptionally strong.

Our dads would take us floundering at night, along one of the local beaches. Flounder are flat fish, brownish on one side and white on the other side. The fish swims along the bottom, with the white side down and has both of its eyes on the brownish side. The flounder would bury up in the sand to hide, in the shallow waters along the shore. We would walk along in the shallow waters, with lanterns for light, in search of the flat fish. We would see other fish, and had to be careful of stingrays, that could stick or cut your feet with the barb on their tails. These barbs were usually a few inches long and serrated on both sides. They were poison, and would really hurt when they cut or poked you in the foot. We would gig flounder with our long handle gigs, which had one or two prongs on the end. We would stick the flounder, then put it on a stringer tied to our belt, and continue our hunt for more flounder. I don't remember gigging a lot of flounder, but we always seemed to find a few. Sometimes we would step on a flounder buried up in the sand, and it would give us a startle. I remember the nights were really calm and peaceful, as we walked along, hearing only the splashes of a few fish, usually mullet, trying to get away from us and our light, which was invading their waters, and the splashing our feet made. Floundering is best in the late summer or fall, when there have been several days with little or no wind, and the water has cleared up a bit so you can see the bottom well. When floundering, we typically walked in about a foot of water and could see the bottom easily.

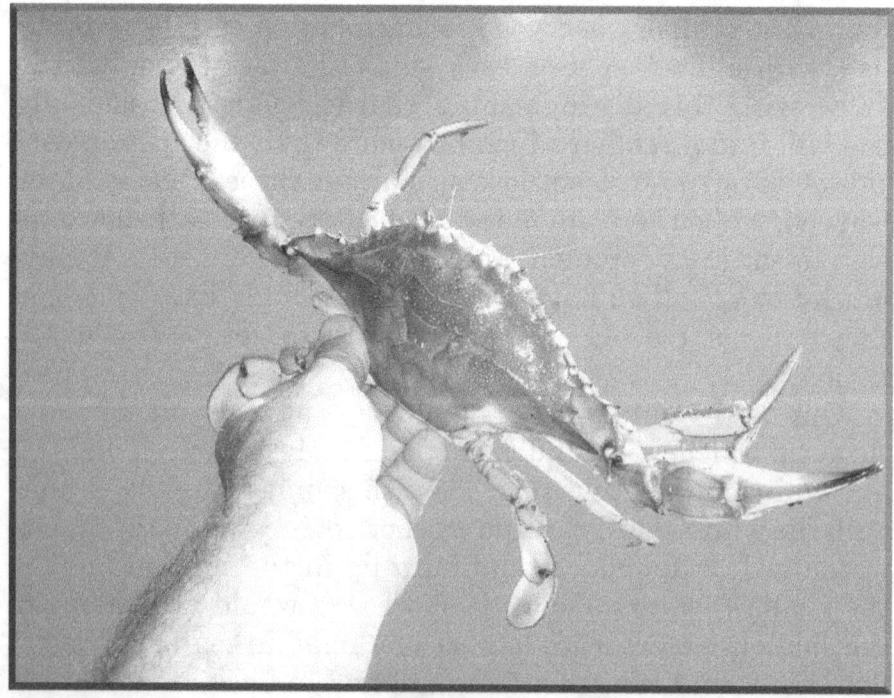

Blue crab

A few blue catfish

Catfish and one redfish (with spot on its tail) in front

Chapter 9
6th, 7th and 8th Grades

When I was in the fifth grade, my mom and dad got a divorce. I guess I was about eleven or twelve, and wasn't a happy camper. My mom, two sisters and I moved to the nearby city of Port Lavaca, another seaport town, which helped because it was close to the water; but it just wasn't the same. I had no friends and no one to play with for a while, and this was a difficult adjustment. I know I was pretty messed up for a while, as I started the sixth grade there in Port Lavaca. I had one teacher who I didn't like much, and I was rowdy both in his class and out. I got regular spankings, and am certain I needed each and every one of them. The teacher was always bringing in a new paddle or yardstick, as he was breaking them regularly over my butt.

I did make a few friends after a while, and I remember one friend, whose little sister was hit by a car on the way to school. We had to walk about six city blocks every day, and there were no sidewalks. One morning she got a little too close to the busy traffic, and was struck. I remember she had a few broken bones, but don't think she had any life threatening injuries. She was taken to the hospital by ambulance, and we were late for school.

My new friends were not into fishing, and all the things I was used to doing with Cousin Steve, so every weekend I insisted I go to Tivoli, though I was not allowed to go there every weekend. I did visit my dad regularly, and got to see Steve from time to time. We had fun doing the things we always did. I did find something really neat to do, which involved a lubricant of some sort, and I spent plenty of time at this new pastime. Suddenly, I wasn't nearly as bored or unhappy.

I continued to visit Steve regularly, and we enjoyed doing the things we did before I was so abruptly moved away. I found out shortly thereafter, Steve had found out about my new pastime, and enjoyed it as much as I did. I remember one camping trip in an old hay barn on our property on the Guadalupe River, when my cousin, another friend and I were bedded down on the floor, with our bb guns and flashlights. We were killing rats and mice that walked the rafters in the barn. It didn't take long to kill out the rats, and not having anything else to do, the three of us indulged in our new pastime in the dark. That was the night I reached puberty. I didn't know my gun was loaded, and didn't even know I had any bullets. It was quite a surprise for me that I did.

My dad would usually pick me up in Port Lavaca and take me to his place. He was not drunk when he picked me up, but was much of the time shortly thereafter. I did not spend much time with him, but instead was out doing things with Steve. I do remember I was really scared when my dad took me home, as he was almost always drunk. I never told my mom because I did not want to end the trips to the ranch. It was dangerous and scary, as most of the trips back home were late Sunday in the dark, but that did not matter as long as we made the trip, which we always did. Once, my dad hit one of the bridge railings on the trip through the Guadalupe River delta. It really messed up the side of his car. That was the only time he hit one of the bridges. The two of us were really lucky he didn't hit one of the oncoming cars or trucks. The bridges were very narrow. I think my mom got wind of his heavy drinking on the weekends, and that he was driving me home drunk much of the time, and tried to put a stop to it. The heavy drinking slowed down, but never quit.

My mom bought a bar to earn a living, when we moved to Port Lavaca, and was quite successful, but didn't spend much time with us kids. We spent a lot of time alone during the week. I studied hard and made good grades, but wasn't having much fun in life there in Port Lavaca. I learned to cook better, as I cooked for myself and my little sister when we got home from school. Sometimes my mom would eat the leftovers, when she got home late at night. My older sister was married by this time, and lived elsewhere. We would get on top of the house at night sometimes, to watch the movie at the local drive-in theater just across the street. We were close enough to hear the outside speakers at the concession stand broadcasting the sound. It wasn't quite like being at the theater, but we enjoyed the movies enough. We seldom had a babysitter, but mom would have a neighbor's daughter, who was a little older than we were, look in on us from time to time. As I was beginning to have some feelings for girls, I thought of this neighbor gal more as a friend than a babysitter. I was about grown up now and didn't need a babysitter, so I thought, and not only tolerated this neighbor, but looked forward to her coming over. She was cute.

My mom was successful enough with the bar, that she opened a second bar across town, and eventually brought in live music, which was a very big success. My mother worked hard and spent long hours taking care of her business. She provided well for us, and we didn't mind her long hours so much after a while. When I got a little older, I would help in the bars sweeping the floors, packing beer in the coolers, and carrying out trash or whatever needed to be done. I didn't spend much time in the bars during business hours though, but did later as I got a bit older. The bars were not bad places for a kid to be, as many might expect. My mom was very strict with rules to keep the places friendly, and catered to the upper class of people in town. They were lawyers, judges, city officials, businessmen and women, and some really smart and influential people around town. All the years she was in business, I can remember only one fight broke out in one of the bars, and it was silenced pretty quick, as some of the attendees of the bar worked for the police department. The fight didn't last long, no damage was caused and it never happened again. That one fight was in the third bar my mom opened, after having such success with the first two. My mom pretty much had a monopoly on the beer business in town. Whiskey was allowed in the bars, but my mom did not sell the hard stuff. She allowed it because she sold a lot of mixers for those who preferred to bring their own hard liquor.

I came to enjoy the bars, as they had shuffleboard and pool tables, and I learned to play the games very well, especially shuffleboard. I could play pool pretty good, but shuffleboard was really big at the time, and there were shuffleboard tournaments several nights a week. I really enjoyed the shuffleboard tournaments. I had a couple buddies, whose moms also worked the bars, so they spent a lot of time in the bars too. The three of us got really good at shuffleboard, and would all play in most of the tournaments. One of us would always win, and if two of us managed to draw each other as partners, we were mostly unbeatable against the grownups. Partners were picked by the luck of the draw. That was the way it was done. One of us kids would always win, and that is one of the ways we made our spending money.

My mom met a man at one of the bars, who came in regularly and whom she would later marry. He lived in my home town of Tivoli, and after they got to know each other a little better, he would help my mom with the bars. I really didn't like him, but don't think I would have liked anyone who would take interest in my mom. He was a good man, and he really didn't interfere with my life so much, so I got to where I could tolerate him being with my mother. I only remember one time when he really bothered me. That was one night after my mom closed the bars, when they came home and he stayed over the night. I was already in bed and was asleep, but was a light sleeper and remember them doing the dirty tango in the bedroom at the end of the very short hallway. I put up a big fuss, as this should never have happened where I could hear what was going on. My mom couldn't be doing this with a strange man, and it was quite disturbing, as I knew what they were doing. It never happened again.

My sister had a girlfriend who would come over to the house quite often. She was a very good looking little gal, just a little younger than me, and for a while I wanted to be a doctor when I grew up. This little neighbor gal would let me practice my doctoring skills on her, and I learned a lot about female anatomy with her. I think she liked my attention to her as much as I did, and she never complained. I hope I didn't screw her up mentally too much, because she really helped me get through a tough time in my life. I totally enjoyed analyzing every square inch of her body, and curing all the life threatening illnesses I imagined that she had. I would see her again, many years later after she was married and working at a local bank. She remembered me quite well, and didn't seem to be messed up by our innocent sexual explorations years earlier, when we were quite young and very inquisitive. Leave young kids alone and you cannot imagine the things they will do. Well, maybe some of you can.

    I played football for a couple years in junior high, and while I enjoyed it, I wish I had taken up golf in the eighth grade, when it was offered for the first time. I didn't because of a peer thing. Playing golf was for sissies, and I didn't want to be labeled as a sissy, so I played football. We were at football practice one day, and the football field was adjacent to the school, when a thunderstorm came up and got severe really quickly. The team was out on the field, when a tornado hit the school. The tornado took off much of the gym roof, and destroyed some of the classrooms. I remember the flying debris over and around the school, and the dry dirt which was stirred up by the high winds stinging my legs below the knees and above the shoes, that was exposed skin. I also remember the coach screaming for us to get on the ground. We were all in full uniform with pads, and that was a good thing, because the smallest kid on the team was picked up and thrown halfway across the field. He was a little shaken up, but not hurt because of the helmet and pads. This was my one and only close encounter with a tornado.

Chapter 10
High School

After three years of school in Port Lavaca, I decided I wanted to go back to school in Tivoli, my home town. My real friends were still in Tivoli, and after much persuasion, I moved in with my dad, who was living with his mother, my grandmother. My grandfather had died when I was only a year old. My dad had sold our old pink brick house after the divorce, and had moved in with my grandmother. She was getting pretty old and needed someone to stay with her, though she didn't really need any help doing anything. I rode my bicycle most of the time, or a horse, or was on foot, but also persuaded my grandmother to let me drive her 1957 Ford. Her car had a standard column shift, and after mastering driving her car, I took driver's education during the summer, after staying the school year with my dad and grandmother. Living in a small town, I drove her car to driver's education many times. I had even driven her car to school a few times.

Staying with my dad and grandmother was a really unique experience. She had a wood frame home, built off the ground about three feet. The three feet between the floor and the ground was plenty room to spend time under the house to get away from it all, or to cool off during the hot summer days. The bridge on the road which ran in front of the house, was over a creek that ran through the ranch, only about two hundred feet from the house. The pink brick house and the wood frame house we originally lived in were just across the creek, so I knew the area very well. I spent a lot of time under that bridge. Water always stood under the bridge, good for catching crawdads, and a good place to play. A huge mulberry tree nearby provided some sweet fruit in the summer.

A chemistry set provided a lot of fun, and I spent a lot of time learning about and mixing many common and some not so common chemicals. I never made any life changing discoveries though. A model airplane didn't last long, as I wasn't very good at flying the plane, but the motor survived the crashes. I put the motor on a plastic dragster. I ran the dragster down a string stretched on the road in front of the house. I spent a lot of time building model cars from the kits I would get as presents. The little gas engine made the light plastic dragster fly down the road at a speed that had to be near the land speed record, but the engine finally failed after numerous really bad crashes.

My grandmother would fix the best homemade bread on Earth. She used a yeast starter which she always kept in a side compartment of the stove/oven. She would usually make two loaves a week, and it got to where I would eat nearly half a loaf when she took it out of the oven. She would always get onto me for wanting to cut the bread too soon. She always said it needed to cool a bit, but I liked it hot as soon as it came out of the oven. It was still warm when the bread was cut, but seldom cut right out of the oven. A little fresh homemade butter on warm fresh homemade bread was heavenly.

That particular winter when I stayed with my grandmother and dad in that old wood frame house, it got pretty cold. I remember waking up several mornings, and there was frost on the floor inside the house. We had gas, but we didn't use it much, except to heat the kitchen and cook meals on the stove. We didn't sleep cold though, as we had some comfy thick feather comforters made with goose down and feathers from the geese we killed. From the time we got out of bed, till we got into the warm kitchen, it did get pretty cold, but what didn't kill us made us tougher right?

While staying with my grandmother and dad, I got my first real job at the local cotton gin. I had worked at one of the local gas stations, picking cotton, and doing some work for a local farmer driving a tractor cutting milo stalks, but the cotton gin job was a real job in my mind, with set hours and good pay. Cousin Steve also got a job at the gin. We worked the sucker pipe, used to suck cotton out of trailers the farmers used to haul the cotton to the gin. We used a tractor to pull the trailers under the sucker pipe, and man-handled the sixteen-inch vacuum pipe that sucked the cotton out of the trailer and deposited it inside the gin, to be processed into bales of clean and seedless cotton. I say we man-handled the sucker pipe because it was one hell of a vacuum cleaner. At times the pipe would man-handle us, and you sure didn't want to get an arm, leg, or some of your clothing into the pipe. It was big enough, that if we were not careful, the pipe could suck us up at least partially into the pipe. We could have been hurt at least to some extent, if this were to happen. We were very careful when operating the sucker pipe and there were no serious incidents.

Two of us usually swapped off working the pipe, and moving the cotton trailers with a tractor, which I had previously learned to drive while I was learning to drive a car. We worked the night shift from seven in the evening until seven in the morning. It was a very long night. Our job was to keep the cotton going into the gin, and the gin never stopped as long as there was cotton to be ginned. There were at times, well over a hundred trailers full of cotton on the yard. We maybe got five minutes at most to eat our late night lunch. The job wasn't really so hard, except when on the sucker pipe, but it was nonstop throughout our twelve-hour shift. The sucker pipe wasn't really all that hard either for us grown kids, as long as we paid attention to what we were doing. If we were not careful enough, the sucker pipe would suck up too much cotton and plug the bottom of the pipe. When this happened, the vacuum created within the pipe would cause the lower outside section of the pipe to suddenly jerk upwards, as the pipe was actually a pipe within a pipe hung on springs. The suction would jerk the pipe upwards and nearly jerk your arms off. We were careful not to do this, but it did happen from time to time. We then had to carefully unplug the pipe to resume our work. The vacuum was never cut off.

I didn't make quite as good grades in Tivoli as I did in Port Lavaca, but I feel I learned more. The curriculum was tougher and the teachers were tougher, but really cared about the students. After the first year of high school in Tivoli, I decided I wanted to finish high school there. The summer I finished driver's education and got my driver's permit, my mother and stepfather got married. They moved to the Guadalupe River, where they would live the rest of their lives. The plot where they moved was directly across the river from where I live now, and have lived most of my adult life. This plot was also two miles from Tivoli, which worked out great, as I moved back in with my mother and stepdad, and went to school in Tivoli. I turned sixteen in the fall and took my driver's test, and got my permanent driver's license.

My stepdad had a 1959 Ford Fairlane with an automatic shift, which I got to drive much of the time. This car was a piece of cake to drive, after driving my grandmother's stick shift. I drove this car quite a bit and considered it my car, as my stepdad had his truck and my mother had her car. I wasn't allowed to go anywhere I wanted, but I did feel like I had a car of my own. The good part was I didn't have to buy the gas for it. But that also meant my mother and stepdad knew how much I was driving. I had to limit my driving as they always kept tabs on how much gas I was burning. I drove to Port Lavaca often, as my mother had the three bars there, and I was getting into the work my mother wanted me to do, not because of the work, but because of the barmaids.

A lot of things were changing in my life now. I was sixteen, and now and the next couple years, things would change a lot. I learned about girls, though I already knew some about them, as I kissed my first girl when I was in the first grade. She didn't like it and I got into trouble. I stayed away from girls for a few years. Then I had that patient who survived all my doctoring in Port Lavaca. I did have a steady girl when I was in the fifth grade, but she didn't last long. I don't know why now, but maybe because I was uprooted and moved to Port Lavaca. Maybe not, maybe it was just me. I don't remember at this point. That was just too long ago.

My mom did not own the land on the Guadalupe River

where she and my stepdad lived, but was allowed to move there because she was the daughter of my grandfather, who had lived on the land for the past twenty-three years. This land, on both sides of the highway, was owned by a man who liked my grandfather a lot, and let him live there rent free due to their friendship. My grandfather and this wealthy landowner had been very good friends for a long time, and when my mother wanted to move there, the wealthy landowner was happy to allow her to do so. My grandfather was on the north side of the highway, upstream as the river flows, and my mother and stepdad were on the south side of the highway. Living with my mother and stepdad, got me farther away from my dad's drinking, where I had easy access to my home town and friends, as well as to Port Lavaca and my mom's bars, I had begun to like spending time in.

I spent a lot of time in Tivoli as well as Port Lavaca during this period, as I had now made many friends in both places. I learned to drink, and though I really didn't like the taste of beer, I consumed at least my fair share. I spent time with all my friends, but the best times were at parties in Tivoli. My mom's barmaids were still a major attraction for me though. Some of them were cousins and my older sister, but some of them were not. They were all good looking and older than me, but age didn't matter. I was always after one or two of them. One of my chores was to take one or two of them home after work from time to time mostly on weekends, but it really wasn't a chore at all with a couple, it was one of the best jobs I ever had.

Living with sisters and a female cousin from time to time, I learned something about bras. This was that back then, they all had the same little hooks and catches in the back of the garment. Some had one catch, some had two, and the ones for the big busted gals had three, but they were basically all the same. I learned how the hooks and catches worked, and I had a little trick that actually surprised a few gals. This trick was I could unfasten the bra with one hand in about half a second. "Well, can I if I can do it with one hand?" For me this was a very easy trick, and I used it to my advantage as often as I could, but we won't go into this any further. This story shall remain my own private story, and some very good memories, as well as a learning experience for me. Bras have many different types of fasteners these days, and can fasten in the front or back, or have no fasteners at all.

I learned to shoot pool, got pretty good, and made some spending money doing so. I would also make some spending money playing in the local shuffleboard tournaments, but shuffleboard was dying out and being replaced by pool, so I got with the program and played a lot more pool. Sometimes I would wait tables, but mostly had to work behind the bar. I only waited tables when my mom was short-handed. Working the bar was easier anyway. I got a lot more practice making change, which is a very good thing to learn, and I learned to do it the old fashion way, not by computer as it is done today.

Tivoli also had its bars, and me and a few buddies would spend a lot of time in one in particular, playing pool and drinking beer, though we were not old enough to do so legally, and playing knock poker in the back corner, before and after closing time. Knock poker was a card game played with dominos that had card faces on them. You start with five domino/cards and would draw an additional card and discard one until you thought you had the best hand. At this time, you would knock the table and the hands exposed. The best hand won the pot. We always played for money. The person doing the knocking didn't always win the pot. The owner was cool with us drinking there and was basically one of us, though he owned the place and was a bit older. He didn't care that we were not old enough to drink, as we were making him money buying beer half the night and sometimes into the early morning hours, which was important for him to stay in business. Sometimes he would close early and lock the door and we would just party the night away.

I remember one night, when we played knock poker in the back corner and drank beer until daylight. A hurricane was blowing outside, but to us it was just another storm. It was a minimal hurricane, but we could literally see the outside wall of the building move in and out with the wind. No one really seemed to be concerned about the hurricane, and we just partied away and had a great time. By early morning, the wind had died down to about fifty mph. Though we drank all night, we never seemed to get drunk. We got out and drove around to see the damage the storm had caused. The damage was minimal.

By today's standards, we would have been considered drunk, 50% of the time. We always drank and drove. School, however, sobered us up a few days. Cops you say? We didn't have cops. We had a deputy sheriff who didn't do much, and certainly didn't bother us. We even had illegal drag races on Saturday night after he went to bed. We knew when it was safe because his daughter was one of us, and took part in the drag races. She would come out after her dad went to bed, so we knew we were OK to have our races down the main highway running through town. We parked at a service station that had closed hours earlier, at the only light in town, a blinker. We drank, played music, danced, and the town was vacant except for us. We had our drag strip marked off, and the races began.

High school days were a lot of fun, but not much of any significance was happening. Just going to school and having fun. I did my studying and made good grades, so I was allowed to do pretty much what I wanted. Mom didn't keep tabs on me very much. We had a party every weekend. Some nights we would park in a vacant service station, and other nights we would gather in a hay field, and drink and dance and play on the round hay bales. Occasionally, someone would have a party at their house, but we seemed to have more fun in a vacant lot or hay field somewhere.

I listened to a lot of music growing up, and really liked a lot of pop and soft rock. I was never a good dancer though. Maybe this was partly because we were dancing in parking lots and hay fields much of the time, and I really didn't have to dance very well. There was music always playing in the bars my mother owned, but there was not a lot of dancing going on, except in one of them where she had live music. This was mostly country music. I did dance there some, but not a lot. Anyway, I did learn to appreciate good music, and later in life have really learned to appreciate country music and classical music. Due to some of my later travels, I have even learned to appreciate some foreign music, especially the music by Ani Lorak, much, but not all of which, is in Russian.

Some of us guys decided to take a road trip one night to Garner State Park, out west of San Antonio, and we left on Friday and came back on Sunday. No one knew we were gone, and no one seemed to care. We were not getting into trouble, and we made it home safe and sound. This is pretty much how things had been most of my life up to now. Cousin Steve and I could have died, or been severely injured more times than I can count, but about the worst that ever happened to either of us was my broken left arm, which considering all that could have happened was no big deal. I just picked myself up and walked to my aunt's house, where I could get some help. One night I cut my hand open on a broken beer bottle and had to have a few stitches, but again, considering all the things that could have happened to us, this was not a big deal.

The only other thing of any significance I can remember about my high school days was my high school sweetheart. She was smart, and in my eyes a very gorgeous gal. I took part in the high school play as leading man, and she was my leading lady. I would not have done the play without her, and I was again thrown into the learning by doing mode. She taught me a little about acting, and I taught her how to French kiss. I don't think I was a great leading man, but it didn't matter. I was learning, and for this book, that is all that matters; always learning by doing. My high school sweetheart was a great gal, and in grade standings she finished just ahead of me by a nose, capturing the title of Salutatorian. I did get recognition as the highest ranking guy. After high school, she went off to San Marcos to attend college, while I attended the local college in Victoria, and we drifted apart.

When I first decided to write this book, it was going to be a self-help book. Then I thought maybe my life could inspire someone to do better, achieve more, to stay out of trouble, to toughen up both mentally and physically and all the while have a generous portion of fun. My life has not been perfect, but I would not change a single thing that has happened to me during my entire life. Can you say the same for your life so far? I have had my fair share of challenges along the way, and I have had my fair share of disappointments, but I have also had a lot of fun in my life, and I continue to have a lot of fun. Life is not going to be fun all the time, and no one's life will ever be perfect, but if you work at staying out of trouble, study in school and also out of school, work hard and follow the good paths, then you can have a great life and reap the rewards life has to offer. You must be mentally strong. Expect that life will not be perfect, and that life will contain many hardships and challenges, but always be positive and optimistic. If you are smart and strive to overcome all obstacles, and look at setbacks as opportunities to learn, you will find your path to success.

There are a lot more cops today. You may not be able to do many of the things I did when I was younger, but there is still a lot of fun to be had without drugs or alcohol, without drag races up and down the main drag in town late at night, or driving without a license. If you listen to your conscience and stay away from people who will get you into trouble, not just <u>even</u> if they call you their friend, but <u>especially</u> if they call you their friend, you will be all right. Real friends do not get friends into trouble. There are so many legal and fun things to do I could never count them all. Use your imagination. I can't tell you what you might like to do, I only know what I like to do, but I bet if you will just use the head on your shoulders, you can think of plenty things you can have fun doing, and stay out of trouble at the same time.

If you are staying in trouble much of the time, or you feel really terrible when you get up in the morning, then you can't really be having fun. Why don't you just try staying out of trouble for once, and wake up in the morning sober instead of hung over, and see what it's like. After a while, you may learn life is not so bad after all. You may find life is worth living, and maybe you have a brighter future. You may find hard work is usually not very much fun, but when a job is finished, and done well, to the best of your ability, the feeling of gratification of not just completing a job, but completing that job well, can be very satisfying. I know I felt good when I made good grades in school and saw good grades on my report card. I felt even better when I showed the report card to my parents. I felt good when I completed a full night's work at the cotton gin, and then another, and another. I felt even better when I got my paycheck for this hard manual labor. I felt good when I crawled on my belly in the marsh, through the mud and the muck sneaking up on some ducks, and was rewarded when I got the ducks I was stalking. If, on the other hand, you are doing things your conscience should be telling you not to do, then you really have a problem. In this case, maybe you should be seeing a counselor. Make the appointment.

I really did have a lot of fun when I was growing up, but that fun included a hefty portion of work. These days I think I am having the time of my life. I still do a little work around the house, but the work portion of my life is a lot less. I am having a lot of less strenuous fun, but the fun is there in a much greater portion, than when I was younger. Again, I am having the time of my life, though I cannot do many of the things I did when I was younger. Fun is what makes life worthwhile, and I hope you can manage to see, the things I did during my life have gotten me to where I am now, and that you can find the right life for yourself along similar lines. Mix work and fun, and if you can find a line of work that is also fun, then you are way ahead of the game. This is why I am telling you just about everything I can remember about my family and my life.

A lot of the fun you will get out of life is from personal gratification, gained through work. Take for example, this book.

While it is work, it is also fun. Writing a book is time consuming, but I have the time. While I hope this book will be a best seller and make me a little money, if it never sells a copy, I will have the personal gratification of writing the book, and will be satisfied I did my best in doing so. I generally need to be motivated to do something like this, and have been motivated by dumb people. While you may not be dumb, maybe you are not as smart as you should be, or can be. Maybe you are just in a rut, and need some motivation. You have motivated me. Now, can I motivate you? If this book will motivate one person, to work harder to create a better life, for him or her, this book will have been worth my effort. Have I motivated you yet? If not, hopefully I will have done so, by the time you finish this book. You are not even to the halfway mark yet.

Chapter 11
Flooding

Well, graduation is over, and this is the beginning of a new chapter in my life. After I got out of high school, it was off to college. Well, not really off; I drove back and forth to school at the community college in neighboring Victoria for two years. I carpooled with some people I went to school with and one or two I did not go to school with, but carpooling is carpooling. I got the first car that was totally mine. It was a used Pontiac, and I got it from a local guy who wanted to get rid of it to buy a newer model. I think it was a 1963 model year, which made it about four years old when I got it. It was big and comfortable and easy to drive with its automatic transmission. It had leather seats and enough room inside to have a party. It also had low mileage and looked like it was well cared for. The car was a pale gold color, which was much better than my grandmother's car and my stepdad's car, which were both ugly shades of green.

Living on the river in a flood prone area, meant sooner or later I would be exposed to flooding. My grandfather had lived for twenty-three years across the highway from where we lived now, and had never had water in his wood frame house. Water had gotten in the yard a few times, but in all, the flooding was minor. Well, luck would have it, in the fall of 1967 when I started college, there was a major flood and it hit us pretty hard. My new car was sitting in the driveway, when my grandfather called us on the phone in the middle of the night. His dog woke him and my step-grandmother up well before daylight with his barking, and my grandfather swung his feet out of bed onto the floor and into water; river water. He called us and woke us up, and the first thing I could think of, was my car sitting in the driveway in the water. I slipped some shorts on, and ran outside and got into the car. I sat down in water, as the water had already almost covered the front seat of the car. The car started, and I backed it up, put it in forward to drive out of the water, toward the highway and higher ground. It died, but once again it started, and off I went. The car was sputtering a little, as water had probably gotten on the ignition and spark plug wires, and the exhaust pipe was under water which muffled the sound. There was a dip in the driveway between the house and the highway, and when I drove through this little dip, the water rushed all the way up to the windshield of the car. The water was over three feet deep and I wasn't sure the car would make it, but finally made it up to dry land on the highway. I stopped and opened the door to let the car full of water drain out. I was really lucky. My mother's car still sat in the driveway the next day as it would not start, and you could not see it, as it was completely submerged in the muddy river water. My stepdad's pickup also sat in the back of the house in the same condition. It would not start either. A little of the top of the truck stuck out of the water.

Hurricane Beulah had hit the area, and while it was not a strong hurricane, it did dump an awful lot of water where we lived, but more importantly upstream. Rain in our local area does not cause flooding, as the water drains very quickly into the river, and then into the bay. But rain falling upstream in our watershed drains into the rivers and streams, and then we get a concentration of water from a very large area coming at us like a wall of water. Now the water does not rise very quickly, as it does in the hill country during a flash flood, but it can and will rise as much as seven to eight inches an hour, usually a day or two after the heavy rain. Not really so quick you can't prepare for the flooding, if you are aware the water is coming, but we were new to the area, and my grandfather had never experienced flooding like this. We were not only not prepared, but not even aware this severe a flood was on its way toward us.

The water got about a foot deep in the house, which was actually a double-wide mobile home, blocked up about three feet off the ground. Other than the vehicles, there was not a lot of damage to our place. We were able to clean up the mess after the water went down. We rented a home in Tivoli while our home was cleaned up. The carpet was replaced, and the paneling walls were cleaned with lemon oil. That oil made them look like new and got rid of all the water stains. We did a lot of cleaning and drying out and salvaged our home, but my grandfather was not so lucky. The highway between our house and my grandfather's house held back a lot of the flood water and acted like a dam, which made the water higher on his side of the highway. The bridges along the highway running through the river bottom, would only let so much water pass through, which kept the water level on our side of the highway lower than on my grandfather's side of the road. Even when the water went over the highway, the water on the downstream side of the highway did not get as high as it did on the upstream side of the road. The water was within a foot of the top of the front door into their house. The house was a total loss and torn down after the water went down. They moved into a mobile home. River people are always river people, and you cannot run us out of the river bottom. Sure we have to put up with rising water from time to time, but there are so many advantages to living here, a little flooding will not deter us.

    This one in 1967, was the first of many floods we would see here on the Guadalupe River. While most of them were not very serious, some were record floods or hundred year floods as they were called, because traditionally one only occurred about once every hundred years. Many floods are attributed to the rains from a hurricane. We pay much closer attention to rainfall upstream from us these days, especially from hurricanes.

    There is always damage caused by flooding, but those of us who have lived here most of our lives, expect the damage, but have learned what to do to hold the damage to a minimum. First of all, you always pay attention to how much it rains upstream and take action when necessary. You need to block up your appliances, put your stuff up high enough to keep it out of the water, you need to spray insecticides for mostly ants and roaches, as they will find their way into your home to get away from the water, and you need a boat for transportation to the highway, or some high ground area where you should have your vehicles parked well before the flood waters arrive. It can rain 25 inches at my home and it will not flood, but the same rain upstream can cause severe flooding. It is always someone else's water causing all our problems. We were new to the river in 1967, as we had only been here a couple years and did not expect this flood, but have learned to watch for and prepare for flooding.

How about another test? I think it is time for another.

What do you call a female calf?

1. A hussy
2. A heifer
3. A holstein

Answer on page 54

What skill did I learn at a Rockport carnival?

1. Throwing darts
2. Eating candy apples
3. Shooting a long bow

Answer on page 57

I hope you are paying a little more attention to what you are reading and got both questions right. If not, you know what you have to do, right?

Flooding 81

It's only ankle-deep, not a problem

We learn to fish around here before we learn our ABCs

Chapter 12
Book Knowledge and Summer Jobs

The next four years I learned a lot, but except for the summer time, mostly it was book learning, not learning by doing. Book learning is good too, even though I would not use what I learned to pursue a career. Much of what I learned will be with me until I die, and I do use some of this knowledge, particularly math, in my everyday life. I chose to be self-employed. I think the most important thing I learned in school, was I didn't want to be cooped up in an office the rest of my life. I think being self-employed requires more knowledge, than is required to work for someone else. Being self-employed requires you to know every detail of the performance of every phase of the business. Most jobs require employees to know only one or two tasks, and very little in the actual running of a business.

While attending college, I worked a summer job with the local pipeline company my dad worked for. They had a summer program for kids of employees who were attending college, and four of us guys worked for them for four summers. This was a job where I learned a lot by doing again. It was a tough job, which not only strengthened the mind, but also the body. Pipeline companies had the job of maintaining the pipelines used to transport crude oil to the refinery for processing, including all the storage tanks and pumping equipment used in this process. This maintenance is what we did. They had a lot of pipelines, and therefore a lot of pipeline leaks which constantly needed repairing. Our job the first couple years was to repair these pipes. For the most part, we were their backhoes, used to dig a hole around the pipes to expose the leaks, so they could be repaired. Our primary tool was a shovel, and we moved a lot of dirt laden with crude oil, for the first couple summers at this job. We dug holes deep, we dug them wide and we dug them long. We dug and dug until the leak was found, and sometimes this took quite a while, and sometimes the holes were quite large. Many of the pipelines were up to three or four feet deep in the ground, and we had to dig the holes usually a foot or two deeper, so we moved literally yards of dirt in search of these leaks. We always found our leak, after which we placed a nigger tit and clamp on the pipe, to temporarily stop the leak until the company welder could come in and make a permanent repair. Sorry folks, but nigger tits are what they were called, a black titty shaped rubber disc, placed over the hole with the pointy side on the hole in the pipe. When compressed by the clamp, it would stop the leak. After the permanent repair was made, we then covered up the hole. This process was hard and dirty work, and as it was a summer job, the work was also very hot, but it was our job so we never complained. We did the job diligently and cheerfully.

The pay was very good at twice the minimum wage at the time, which meant we were making $2.50 an hour. This wouldn't be much these days, but for us kids it was a really good wage. We worked several counties and when we were not making repairs to pipelines, there were always an endless supply of other maintenance tasks to perform, like mowing the yards at some of the pump stations, breaking apart and cleaning valves and other pipe connections, and performing maintenance on the vehicles.

After a couple summers of leak repairs, we learned the area pretty well, and knew where most of the companies' property and responsibilities were located. At times we were given a vehicle to drive to our assigned tasks. We performed some of the work in teams of usually two of us four guys. We also walked pipeline rights-of-way looking for pipeline leaks, and this was sometimes through heavy brush. Sometimes we walked for miles in search of leaks. We were dropped off at one road, and we walked the right-of-way until we got to another road, where we could be picked up. Sometimes it was quite a distance to the next road, and at times the rights-of-way were so overgrown with brush, we could not even tell where the right-of-way was.

Our boss was about the same age as my dad, and was brutal. He would really get mad at us kids, when we didn't do things like he wanted. He would show us what he wanted done, and how he wanted it done, by doing it himself for a few minutes. Then, he would hand the tool to us, and stood and watched us do the task with a red face, a look like he was going to have a heart attack, if we didn't do the job right. While he was tough on us, he got more out of us kids than he would have otherwise, and we learned to do things better over the years. He demanded our respect and got it. We certainly learned "righty-tightie; lefty-loosie" when it came to tightening and loosening bolts.

By the fourth year, he lightened up a little. I even saw him smile a time or two. He was just trying to get the most effort out of us kids. We now knew the area, and the work we were supposed to do, about as well as we were going to learn, and were given our own truck, the oldest and most beat up truck in the fleet, to drive to most of the tasks we were assigned. We were told what to do, where to do it, and we got the job done. Much of what we did this last year was painting, and the company began hiring backhoes again, to dig out pipeline leaks. This is what they did before we started our summer job. More leaks could be fixed faster that way, but probably at a higher cost, but there didn't seem to be quite so many leaks now, and we had other things to do. We painted pumping units and exposed pipeline connections, and everything had to be a specific color. Motors and their covers were painted Leroy green, suction line valves were fire engine red, discharge line valves were black, and pipes in between were silver. The pipes and valves were easy to paint, but the motors were usually covered with oil and grease, and had to be scraped and thoroughly cleaned before painting. This was the big chore, as some of the motors were really, really nasty with oil, grease, and dirt.

After two years at the local college, I graduated with good grades, but no honors. I excelled at math, where I got a perfect score in one of the classes—trigonometry. The professor told me he had never had anyone make 100% on a final, in any of his previous classes. My class average for the semester was only 99% though. I got into literature a bit during the last year, and enjoyed the poetry of Edgar Allen Poe, and William Shakespeare's plays very much. Biology was OK too. I did well at live surgery on a toad, but the patient was killed at the end of the class. It made a good demonstration.

After graduation, I celebrated with my friends, then worked through the summer and prepared for college at a distant university. I would attend two years at the university at Kingsville, which was about a hundred miles away. I could not carpool this distance, so I stayed in a dormitory the first year. Kingsville was a dry land city, hot most of the time, but overall a fairly decent place to stay. A few things were quite memorable. The rough roads that were continually patched, felt like driving over rough cobblestone. The city was never prepared for the sudden downpours during the rainy season, and the streets flooded often. There were no storm drains. There was a restaurant called the Day & Night. This place really served up some fantastic Mexican food. I ate there often with a couple buddies, usually late at night, until it was closed down by the Health Department, due to too many roaches in the kitchen. I did a lot more partying in Kingsville, and I probably spent too much time at the local titty bars, but that was a long time ago and there is nothing I can change about that now. Anyway, I did learn a few things, though I probably killed off a lot of brain cells with alcohol, during my two years there. So far I have mostly tried to teach you a few things I have learned by doing. Hopefully, you are also learning to *not* do some of the things I was doing. I hope you know which things these are.

Learning from books covers such a broad range of subjects, you can learn things from books you will never learn by doing things yourself. You may not think you will ever use the stuff you learn in books, and some of this may be true, but for the most part, you will use the knowledge you get from books and teachers the rest of your life. You will learn to speak better, be better able to carry on a good conversation, and maybe, just maybe, you will understand what people are talking about, when they happen to be smarter than you. People will know you are educated, and they will certainly know when you are not. A good education is so important, and whether you think you will use it or not, the higher education you can attain, is well worth the effort. My education is important to me, though I cut it short before getting a Bachelor's Degree. Stay in school as long as you can. You will be rewarded by doing so. Math is especially important. I went all the way up to level three advanced calculus, which totally went over my head. I don't think you really need this stuff in everyday life, but you should try to at least get through a couple years of algebra. This is very important, as is geometry. A little chemistry is always good too. I took mostly organic chemistry, and since most of what we see in everyday life is organic, organic chemistry is very important.

To know you are a carbon I based unit, and that all organic compounds contain carbon is important. If you burn a carbon based material, it will turn black, and if you burn it completely, what is left is black powder. This powder is carbon. Nitrogen (N) is also important in our chemistry, and the atmosphere is made up mostly of nitrogen. The nitrogen in the air is not soluble in water, in other words, it does not dissolve in water, and cannot be used by plants. Nitrogen is important in plant growth, and lightning turns non-soluble nitrogen into soluble nitrogen, so it can be used by plants. In other words, lightning produces fertilizer for plants. A common use of nitrogen these days, is in freezing foods quickly, particularly seafood. Nitrogen is compressed and liquefied, and the seafood is immersed in this liquid on stainless steel conveyors. The liquid nitrogen is below fifty degrees below zero, and will freeze the food very quickly.

Along with nitrogen, potassium (K) or potash, one of several potassium containing salts, and phosphorus (P) are also very important to plant life, and are contained in most fertilizers. Potash is a common name for some mined or man-made salts, which contain potassium in a water soluble form. Magnesium (M), Calcium (Ca) and other trace elements may also be contained in some fertilizers. Calcium is the primary component in bones that makes them hard. Anhydrous ammonia (NH_3), which is anhydrous because it does not contain water, was commonly used in years past to enhance the growth of commercial plants, because of the soluble nitrogen in the ammonia. It is not used much around here anymore, and there are many ways to get nitrogen into the soil for commercial plantings. If ammonia were not anhydrous, it would likely be ammonium hydroxide with a chemical formula of NH_4OH, because it contains water (H_2O). You may be familiar with the strong odor of ammonia and ammonium hydroxide.

Carbon, oxygen (O), hydrogen (H), sulfur (S), and nitrogen are elements. Elements are the basic building blocks of everything organic and inorganic. There are currently 118 known elements on the periodic table of elements, and these elements are made up of atoms, the smallest whole unit of existence of organic and inorganic chemicals. In the case of carbon, one atom of carbon is also one molecule of carbon. In the case of oxygen, it takes two atoms of oxygen to make one molecule of oxygen (O_2), as it exists naturally. An atom consists of protons (+), neutrons (neutral) and electrons (-) that circulate around the central protons and neutrons, much like the earth and other planets revolve around the sun. Many elements are well known, but some are rare and others manmade. The rare and man-made elements are important, but in everyday life are not important. I don't even know some of them, and it is not important for me to know them all. Other important everyday elements are sulfur, a yellow naturally occurring element, and copper (Cu) from which pennies and copper pipe is made. Sulfur is not harmful in moderation, and you will find it in water, the ground and petroleum products. Iron (Fe) is also very common, as are silver (Ag) and gold (Au). Iron ore from the ground is used to make iron and steel. Iron and steel oxidize to form rust. They turn a reddish color, because as it oxidizes, the iron molecules combine with oxygen to form a new molecule, iron oxide (FeO). Iron oxide is reddish. This is a chemical reaction. There are many chemical reactions which occur naturally, as well as many that are forced to occur by man, to create something new. Many chemical reactions can be made to occur faster, by adding a chemical catalyst. This catalyst is often some type of mild acid. Heat can also be used to speed up a chemical reaction.

Molecules are mixtures of elements, and can be naturally occurring or man-made. Molecules include water, ammonium hydroxide and ammonia above, salt (NaCl) which is made up of the elements sodium (Na) and chlorine (Cl), and carbon dioxide (CO_2). Sodium is a heavy and dangerous metal, and chlorine is a deadly green gas, but when chemically combined, they form salt our bodies cannot do without. Our body uses oxygen when we inhale, and gets rid of carbon dioxide when we exhale. Plants basically do the same thing in reverse. Plants take in carbon dioxide and give off oxygen. Chlorophyll is a molecule, which all green plants contain. It gives them their green color, and aids in the process of producing oxygen, and turning sunlight into energy for the plant to live. Plankton is tiny plants that live in the oceans, and this is where we get most of the oxygen on this planet. This is something you should think about, every time you hear about an oil spill. I've gotten into biology a little, but that's all right, organic chemistry and biology are both intertwined.

Some other chemical molecules include alcohols, the most common of which is ethanol (CH_3CH_2OH), is the alcohol produced by the fermentation of grapes and some other plants. This is the alcohol in wine, whiskey, and beer. It is also the alcohol used in extending gasoline in your vehicles, most of which is made from corn. Alcohols are mostly flammable liquids. Both flammable and inflammable mean something will burn. Something combustible will burn as well. Noncombustible and nonflammable mean something will <u>not</u> burn. One hundred proof alcohol products contain 50% pure alcohol. This is just the way it is measured in alcoholic drinks. Pure alcohol is 200 proof, but it can only exist naturally as 190 proof, or 95%

alcohol, because it will absorb water from the air. There are many different alcohols. If you choose to drink alcohol, you should not drink anything but ethanol. Drinking the others may result in death or blindness. Benzene (C_6H_6) is important, because it is a cancer causing chemical. I messed with it a little in college, as sodium was stored in benzene, because sodium reacts violently and even explosively with water. Benzene is a carbon ring. The molecule contains the carbon atoms in a continuous ring, and the hydrogen atoms float around this ring, and are not specifically attached to any one carbon atom. Stay away from benzene if you can.

Acetylene (C_2H_2) is a more complex molecular gas, in that it has a triple bond between the two carbon atoms. It is worth mentioning, because it is used to burn a cutting torch used in welding. The triple bond is caused by a process that removes four atoms of hydrogen from the molecule. A carbon atom has four bonding places, at which other atoms can attach. I will not dwell on the more complex molecules, but this one is common and deserves mentioning. Also worth mentioning, is if you are around someone welding, know that looking at the welding arc can burn your eyes very quickly. If you are close to the person welding, severe eye burn can occur in a matter of seconds.

There are many, many extremely complex molecules. If you want to see complex molecules, see a chemistry textbook. Propane ($CH_3CH_2CH_3$) is a common fuel gas, used in household heating and cooking. Some gasses can be compressed under high pressure, and they will liquefy. Propane, carbon dioxide, and nitrogen, are some common gasses that are liquefied. These liquids are very cold, and will freeze anything they come into contact with. They also vaporize quickly, when removed from their container, and are no longer pressurized. Compressed liquids can be transported by truck, much more efficiently than can gasses. Propane, as a liquid compressed gas, will vaporize when the pressure is reduced through a regulator, and burned in a furnace, cook stoves, and ovens. A little liquid propane will produce a lot of vapor, and will burn for a long time in a stove or furnace. It is a clean burning and efficient gas for this purpose. It is also used as a clean fuel in some vehicles. Carbon dioxide can be further pressurized and cooled, and will solidify. This solid CO_2 is commonly known as dry ice. Dry ice is dry, because when CO_2 evaporates, it goes directly from a solid to a gas, a process called sublimation, unlike water which goes from a solid (ice) to a liquid (water) to a gas (water vapor). Ice will drip water as it melts, while dry ice gives off carbon dioxide vapor.

Finally, sugar, one of the most common of which is D-glucose ($C_6H_{12}O_6$), and also known as dextrose or grape sugar, is a compound that is among my favorites, along with sucrose, as they are used to sweeten many of my favorite foods. Sugar is produced as a liquid, and then dehydrated by removing the water, leaving sugar crystals. Sugar is made from grapes, sugar beets and sugar cane to name a few. The sugar molecule is relatively complex, and there are several different kinds of sugar with similar molecular configurations, which designate them as sugars.

One last bit of information dealing with chemistry, there are two main temperature scales. In the centigrade scale I, the freezing point of water is 0° C and the boiling point of water is 100° C, at sea level. In the Fahrenheit scale (F), the freezing point of water is 32° F and the boiling point of water is 212° F, at sea level. There is a third scale, called the Kelvin scale (K). The centigrade degree plus 273 will give you the Kelvin degree measurement. This scale is not used often. I might add, above sea level; let's say if you go into the mountains, water boils at less than 212° F. This is due to the lower atmospheric pressure in the mountains.

Before I move on to the next subject, Biology, I would like to mention, English was my worst subject in school. You may notice my use of the English language in this book is not perfect. If that is the case, you are probably a little smarter than the people for which this book was written. If not for computer spelling and grammar check, it could have been much worse. If English is your strong suit, you are probably book smart in other areas too, and do not need much of the information I am giving you. But some of the things in this book, you cannot learn from a textbook. If you are a city person and dropped into a forest and forced to try to survive on your own, my guess is you will die. You may need this book more than the dumb people for which it was written. You may actually learn something anyway. Maybe you are reading my book for its entertainment value. Whatever the reason, I thank you for reading my book, and hope you enjoy my work.

Chapter 13
Plants

Biology is the study of plants and animals, and includes botany and zoology that separates biology into the study of plants and animals, respectively. It is important to know what kinds of plants grow around you. It is important to know which are edible, which are not, which are useful in other ways, and it is also important to know which ones can hurt you, through dangerous chemicals they contain such as poison ivy, poison oak, poison sumac and mushrooms. Others have thorns, like cat claw shrubs, mesquite trees, lemon trees and cactus. Some are beneficial in treating skin problems, like aloe vera shoots. Probably most importantly, however, are those that provide food. We should all know the garden varieties, and if you don't know these, you can find them in most garden and seed catalogs. They are numerous and very tasty when fully ripe. I grow many types of fruit, as I like fruit more than veggies in most cases. Varieties I grow include numerous types of plums, peaches, pears, nectarines, citrus and some pecans, though this is a nut, as well as banana trees. There are many other varieties, but some may not grow well in your area. If you grow fruit and vegetables, it is important to know what varieties are suitable for your area and your climate. A seed catalog will tell you this. If you don't have a garden, try starting a small one. If you don't have the room, try a few pots. There are also vines like grapes, dewberries, blackberries and raspberries that produce tasty and healthy fruit. Dewberries and muscadine grapes grow well in my area, and grow in the wild in many areas. Others can be grown, but do not produce well here. These days, with genetics and grafting, however, some varieties may grow virtually anywhere.

Vegetables I grow include corn, beets, carrots, onions, potatoes, cantaloupe, and green beans. Some varieties of vegetables grow better in cooler climates, or the cooler time of the year, like beets, potatoes, carrots, lettuce, cabbage, broccoli, and cauliflower. Other varieties, do better in the warmer time of the year, like watermelon, cantaloupe, corn, tomatoes, squash, and cucumbers. It is important to know what varieties you can grow, and what time of the year you can grow them, as not all vegetables can be sown early in the year, and you must wait until the weather and ground warms up to the proper temperature, for the seeds to germinate. To get an early start with your garden, some may be germinated inside, then transplanted outside when the weather warms up and the risk of frost is gone. I like to grow a garden in the fall, as well as the spring.

 I would like to share one recipe with you, for one of my favorite veggies. That favorite is pickled beets. Detroit Dark Red is the best variety. Mature beets are harvested, washed and the tops cut off leaving about an inch of top, and boiled in a large pot until soft inside. You can tell by poking a few with a toothpick. After cooking, drain the hot water and add cool water. Then cut off the ends, and the peeling comes off very easily under a cool running water faucet. The peeled beets are then cut into chunks, about an inch in diameter, and set aside. In another large pot, add equal parts of sugar, vinegar (9% acidity) and water. Depending upon the number of beets, add one cup sugar, one cup vinegar, and one cup water, or multiples of this amount of these ingredients. Make certain you have enough juice for all the jars. Also add some whole cloves, maybe a tablespoon or two, depending upon the number of beets. Bring this liquid to a boil. Taste the liquid to check for sweetness and tartness due to the vinegar. Adjust if necessary. I usually add a little extra vinegar and sugar to make a stronger mix. Add the cut beets to this boiling liquid, and bring back to a boil. Heat the jar lids in boiling water to sterilize, and make the lids seal easier. Do this while waiting for the beets to boil. When the beets are again boiling, cut off the heat and scoop the beets into sterile clean jars, and add juice to within a quarter inch of the top. Make sure you get a few cloves in each jar. Do this quickly while the beets are very hot. Clean the rim of each jar with a damp cloth, add lid and ring, and tighten to seal. Set the jars on the counter to cool. They should be ready to eat in a couple weeks. Refrigerate before eating, as they are best chilled, and after opening the jars, unless you eat them all. I usually eat them up pretty quickly.

Trees native here, that do not produce food, but are good for firewood and shade are ash, mesquite, elm and cedar elm trees, which I use for firewood, and also cypress, hackberry, willow and box elder trees, which are not quite as good for firewood. I also grow honeysuckle for its sweet aromatic smell, and crepe myrtle for its pretty flowers. The grass growing in my yard is mostly carpet grass, aka St. Augustine, and I say mostly because there is also Gordo bluestem, coastal Bermuda, native Bermuda, and numerous other flowering weeds, and even a little poison ivy and poison sumac. Poison ivy, oak and sumac have three leaves, and are easily identified by their three leaves. Poison sumac has waxy leaves. All three are vines that will tend to grow up trees, but can also be found scattered over the ground. These are young and immature plants, but can hurt you nevertheless. Dead or dormant vines with no leaves can give you a rash. If you are out in the brush, you should know what these plants look like, and try to avoid them. Sometimes this may be impossible.

I grow purple Jew or creeping Jew, a low growing ground cover plant, which I grow around the perimeter of my home. It is a pretty plant with tiny pink flowers at times. The reason I grow it, is that it is a very tough, durable and easy plant to grow, and I grow it in areas where other plants I have tried, haven't survived. It can be mostly purple to mostly green, depending on how much water it is getting. When very dry, it will be mostly purple, but will green up quickly when it gets a good watering. I don't think a drought can kill the stuff; it is that tough.

I grow parsley, garlic, dill and green onions, which I use in my cooking, but don't grow a lot of herbs, because I do not know how to use them in my cooking, and don't really care for many of their flavors. It is just too easy to buy spices, and spice mixtures at the grocery store. I can find good spice mixtures I like, without all the fuss of growing and mixing them myself. Home grown herbs do taste better, but several professional mixtures have worked well for me. For the most part, I use fresh green onion, fresh garlic and garlic powder, and a lot of it, salt, black pepper, cumin, several celebrity rubs and mixes, an Italian mix, and a Greek mix. Occasionally, I will also use nutmeg and cinnamon. Spices are really good for you, especially onion and garlic, and will make many foods taste much better. I use so much garlic, that if you were to cut me, I would likely bleed garlic.

There are some plants that grow on, and attack the trees in my area. Mistletoe grows in many of the trees around my home. It attacks and draws energy from the trees. Mistletoe will eventually kill some trees, but elm, cedar elm, and cypress are fairly resistant. Mistletoe will attack and kill hackberry trees, and is very hard on ash trees, but has a more difficult time killing the ash trees. Ball moss will also attack and kill trees, and while it is in some of the trees around my home, it is mostly in the cedar elm. It seems to like these trees, but the ball moss really likes live oak trees, and you will find a lot more of it where there are more live oak trees. I do not have any on my property near my home. Spanish moss is in some of the trees around my home, but appears to not damage the trees. There is also some other fungi and mold on the trees around my home, but they do not appear to be causing any damage. I did get some kind of black smut fungus on my tangerine tree, and it killed it. It covered the tangerine tree, and then killed the tree very quickly. I really liked this tree, and it was just getting mature enough to produce a large crop of tangerines. I will try another in the spring, as I really love tangerines fresh and their squeezed and chilled juice. Another lesson learned, and I hope I can prevent the next tangerine tree from getting killed.

Numerous vines and woody plants grow around my home,

like wolf weeds and wild hibiscus, and so many more which I do not know the names of, but it is not important to know the names of all of them. You should know the names of most of the plants growing in your area. Why? To be a little smarter than the next guy if nothing else. It is not absolutely important to know the names of all of them.

There are always a lot of honey bees around, as I have many flowering vegetables and fruit trees, as well as ornamentals. Bees are very important in the pollination of plants, so they will produce fruit. Killer bees have also migrated into my area, but I have seen no evidence of these aggressive bees to date. I do need to keep an eye out for them, as they can be very dangerous. Thus far, they have not been a problem, but I continue to keep a lookout for them, and so must you if you live in an area where they may exist. Don't kill honey bees indiscriminately though, as they are very useful and necessary to the well-being of your fruiting plants. The honey these bees produce is the only food that will not spoil. It may crystallize and grow mold, but it will not spoil. That should just about do it for the biology lesson.

My garden

Cantaloupe on the vine

Fresh corn-on-the-cob and new potatoes

Freshly harvested beets, ready for pickling

Chapter 14
Birds and Animals

Numerous birds and animals live around, or frequent my home. There is a family of wrens, small brown birds that live around my back porch, and I see them regularly, hunting for bugs or drinking out of the pan under my miniature rose bush pot. There are also a few hummingbirds that frequent the area, and I put out a feeder for them, when I see them around here. The little wrens and hummingbirds are pleasing to watch, as they go about their everyday lives. There are also some cardinals, chickadees, and vireos that frequent my place, as I keep birdseed in a tray on the back porch railing. Most birds are migratory and will not stay here throughout the year. Birds migrate to stay away from bitterly cold weather and to hunt for food, which is not available in all areas throughout the year. Some migrate to safer nesting grounds far north, where man is scarce. Others have shorter migration routes. Birds generally migrate from north to south in the fall, and then back north. Some birds can tolerate colder temperatures more than others. Hummingbirds cannot tolerate the cold weather geese and ducks can, simply due to the difference in their size. Goose feathers and down, provide about an inch of very dense insulation. Hummingbirds have, at best, an eighth inch of protection.

Squirrel, raccoon, gopher, opossum and armadillo are some of the pesky animals that frequent my yard. I try to keep them eradicated, but they consistently eat my fruit in spite of all my efforts to keep them out, and root up my yard in the case of the armadillo and gopher. We have red squirrel, and they are smart, fast, and difficult to eradicate. Armadillo, raccoon and opossum are nocturnal; they come out at night, and I have spent a lot of nights hunting them in my yard. Raccoons are difficult to catch in the yard, and are very fast and have keen eyes. I also have a live trap to catch the raccoons, and this is an easier method to catch them. I have caught opossum in the live trap too. I have even had bobcat, wild hogs and deer in the yard. This is rare and I have not killed any of these critters in the yard, but see signs of them from time to time. If I can catch a hog especially, or the deer that has been rubbing the bark off some of my shrubs in the front yard with his antlers, I just may have to take them out. We will eat them, and they will make quite a few very tasty meals. Deer meat is good, but I actually prefer a big fat wild hog.

There is always a snake or two around, and we have four poisonous varieties around here. Those varieties are copperhead, rattlesnake, coral snake and cottonmouth. We also have harmless garter and grass snakes. The copperhead is a small reddish and tan snake, with a big head for its body size. Its color varies a bit with location and diet, but if you run across one of these, you had better know what they look like, and that they are poisonous. The coral snake is similar to the king snake, in that they have red, black and yellow stripes around the length of its body. The coral snake has a small head, and it is difficult for it to bite you, but can get you on the finger or other small area of your body, where it can get some skin into its small mouth. The coral snake can be differentiated from the king snake, by which color touches another color. Remember "red on black, friend of jack," meaning it is not poisonous, and "red on yellow, kill a fellow," meaning this is the coral snake, and can kill you if given the chance.

I had some trouble with my air conditioning unit once, and while the technician had the top off the condenser, the outside portion of the unit, I decided to clean the leaves out of the bottom of the unit. I reached in and grabbed a hand full of leaves, and to my surprise, there was a small copperhead in this bunch of leaves. The little snake bit me on the hand near the thumb. The little critter only caught me with one of its two fangs, and injected me with very little of its poison, but it did make me sick for a day or so. I took a couple ibuprofen tablets, and did not go to the doctor. I was fine in a couple days. If it had been a grown snake, and had injected me with more venom, it would have been a different story. So far, this is the first and only time a snake has bitten me.

Rattlesnakes usually have diamond shapes on their brownish, black and yellowish bodies. These snakes have big heads, and are easy to recognize. They will rattle the rattler on their tail if you get close, or they get pissed off. The sound their tail rattler makes is very distinctive. If you hear one, you will know you are in trouble, and about to get bitten. The cottonmouth is a water snake, also called a moccasin or water moccasin. They are dark brown to almost black. They are large with big heads, and will bite you without warning, unlike the rattlesnake with its warning rattle. They are often called water moccasins, because they always live around the water, but adding water to their name is not appropriate, though the dictionary says otherwise, as they are simply moccasins or cottonmouths. They get their cottonmouth name, because the inside of their mouth is white like cotton.

Since I live on a river delta, there are numerous water birds, or at least birds that frequent the river for water or to hunt for food. There are kingfishers, cranes, herons, roseate spoonbills, ibis and egrets. The great blue heron is a large bird that feeds primarily in the river and marsh. I see them often. Egrets are white and also feed around the water and around cattle. They are known as cowbirds, and will feed on ticks and other bugs that get on cattle. The whooping crane's primary nesting ground is not far from my home, at the Aransas National Wildlife Refuge. They come here every winter. The Sandhill crane is gray in color, and similar to the white whooping crane in size and shape. It is more common than the whooping crane, and can be found in the marsh, and occasionally in pastures, feeding on bugs and whatever. They have a very distinctive cackle, and once you hear it, you will always know when a Sandhill crane is around sounding off. Of course, we also have alligators that are all too common in the area, and pose a real and deadly threat from time to time, near my home. This threat is dealt with in an appropriate manner. My

.22 magnum with hollow point ammunition works quite well.

There are too many smaller critters to name, which get quite thick around the house at times, but some of the more common include chameleon and geckos. I have been trying to eradicate the geckos for some time without success, because I do not like them. They leave quite a mess in the attic, as well as outside, with their droppings. The chameleon on the other hand, I like. They do not make such a mess. They like to be outside where they are supposed to be, and they are pretty. They change colors from shades of green to shades of brown, according to what they are trying to blend in with. There are almost always a few mosquitos, and at times there are a lot of these very aggressive blood sucking insects. When it is very hot and dry, and when it is very wet, they are not so bad, but when it is in between, and there are periods of rain and dry, they can get quite thick. They can get so bad around here, you are best not to be going out at night, when they swarm. There is really no way to avoid mosquitos, when you live in a marsh. There are crickets, termites, fire ants, flying ants, moths, butterflies, gnats, webworms, grasshoppers, earthworms, crawfish, mice, Norway rats, asp, beetles, common flies, fruit flies, roaches, silverfish, mayflies, wasps, walking sticks, yellow jackets, and locust to name a few I see on a regular basis. Some are pests at times, but most of these you can never completely eradicate. The best I can do is to try to keep them out of the house. This is never totally possible either.

There are some critters that are extinct, or virtually nonexistent around here. There are no more horny toads and jack rabbits, or at least I have not seen any for many years. Cottontail rabbits are few and far between, as are red ants. While there are still a lot of geese and ducks, they do not number in the millions around here like they did when I was younger. I have not seen any quail lately either. There are some species that are more plentiful. There are more deer and there are more redfish. The TP&WD has worked hard to increase the deer population, but I think most of the work has been done by ranchers, as this is beneficial for all the deer hunters around. They also worked hard to increase the number of redfish, because they are a very popular game fish. They started a breeding program for redfish many years ago, when they thought there was a need for more of these fish, when there was actually no shortage of redfish. Then one year, we had an extended period of very cold weather, and millions of redfish were killed. They found out there were really a lot more redfish than they thought, and the real problem was with the dumbasses trying to catch them. There was no real shortage of the fish, but after the freeze, the program was really needed. They have now carried this program to the extreme, and there are once again too many redfish. If you overpopulate any one variety, it is always at the expense of other varieties. This is why Cousin Steve and I always killed a lot of nongame animals along with the game animals. We kept a balance amongst all the critters. The folks at the TP&WD do not understand this. City folks!

The river that runs behind the house contains three main varieties of catfish, blue cat, yellow cat and channel cat. The blue cat is bluish and white with whiskers, and is a very tasty meal. They grow to around 50 pounds here, and are not very good eating when they get that big, as they get very fat, and the fat makes them have a strong fishy taste. Of course some people like the fishy taste, including me, but you can get all the fishy taste you want in the fish up to around 20 pounds. The bigger fish are best left for breeding stock. The normal fish we catch weigh from a pound to eight pounds. They are the best to eat, and easier to process than the bigger fish. The yellow cat, or flathead catfish, grows up to around 100 pounds, and is very good eating in the five to twenty-five-pound range. They are yellowish to dark gray, and have a flat head and whiskers as well, as do all catfish. They are usually caught on live bait, perch being the bait most often used. The channel cat is a yellowish and black fish with tiny black spots on much of its body, and generally do not grow much over eight pounds. The meat of the channel cat is generally a little yellowish. The channel cat is a fishy, muddy tasting fish in the wild, but is the most common variety grown in fish farms. The food used in fish farms to feed these fish, and the fact that they are harvested at around the two-pound range, takes much of the fishy muddy taste out of the fish. There is also another little catfish in the river called the bullhead, but it is rare and not a good eating fish, though all catfish can be eaten. The bullhead is just not a choice fish, and is greenish, has a big head compared to the rest of its body, and spends much of its life in the calm shallow stagnant waters. The channel cat also spends much of its time in the more stagnant waters, and that is likely the cause of its muddy taste, because of its diet found in the stagnant waters. I don't usually keep them when I am fishing.

Other fish in the river include three main varieties of gar, the alligator gar, the needle-nose gar and the spotted gar. Spotted gars do not grow very large, but the needle-nose gar will grow up to around 50 pounds, and has needle sharp teeth on its long narrow nose. The alligator gar is the king of the gar in the river, and grows to over 200 pounds, and around seven feet long. It is basically an alligator without legs, and can hurt you very badly with its big teeth, if it can get hold of you.

Another notable fish is the buffalo, a sucker fish much like a giant perch. A sucker fish has no teeth. It has a soft mouth, good for sucking algae off rocks, or whatever. These fish currently overpopulate the Guadalupe and San Antonio rivers, and should be controlled, but the TP&WD will not allow this, as nets are required. Nets are the plague to the TP&WD. The morons! Buffalo grow to around 25 pounds, and is a trash fish like gar. We also have carp, another trash fish. Carp are similar to buffalo, only longer and slimmer, and is yellowish green in color. Most fish have many shades of several colors, and it is difficult to describe them by color alone. I have eaten both gar and buffalo, and they are not bad, just not choice fish to eat. All these fish have scales, unlike catfish which have smooth, slimy skins. Actually gar has a cross between scales and a skin, much like an alligator. There are thousands of other critters, large and small living in this river, as with most rivers. It would be impossible for me to list them all here, but the more common include grass shrimp, that don't grow much over an inch long, freshwater shrimp that grow to about a pound, crawfish, perch, snapping turtles, soft shell turtles which are very tasty but really messy to process, minnows, water bugs, and leaches. These days, there are also a couple varieties of fish in the river that should not be here. These are tilapia and piranha. I do not know how these species got into the river, but not likely by natural methods. They are not a problem yet, but I would bet money, one day they will cause real problems.

In addition to the freshwater varieties of critters, there are also saltwater critters that migrate into the river at times, and these varieties include redfish, mullet, shad, blue crabs, and occasionally even saltwater catfish (hardheads), flounder, stingray, shrimp, eel and trout. These fish and crustaceans will migrate to wherever they need to find food, and protect themselves from heat and cold. They can tolerate brackish water that exists between the saltwater and the freshwater, and some saltwater species even need the brackish or freshwater to grow their young, which then migrate back to the saltwater when they mature.

I hope I am not boring you too much. Sometimes learning is boring. I will try to keep the story interesting, but sometimes that may not be possible, especially if you are not really used to learning new things. I am giving you information every step of the way, and you can remember it, or not. That is up to you. I will try to teach you some common everyday things in an interesting manner. What you do with the information is up to you. You should take charge, learn and do what you need to do, to make your life happy, rewarding and fulfilling. But will you? I have been told, and have learned, there is only one person on this planet that can make you happy, and that person is YOU. Your life is, and always has been, in your hands. What you do with it, is up to you.

People make excuses for why their life has turned out how it has turned out, but the fact is every person on this planet has the power to control their destiny. The more you know the more power you have over that destiny. So, do what you want, but I am trying to teach you a few things. Whether or not you will ever use any of the stuff I am trying to teach you, I don't know. But I guarantee you one thing though, and that is when you finish and absorb the information I have chosen to include in this book, you will know more, and you will be smarter than you were before. You will also be stronger and more mentally capable of changing and directing your destiny in the direction you want it to go, should you take my advice. You have the power within you, and if you are mentally strong and dedicated to your future, you can achieve whatever it is you wish to achieve. Whether or not you choose to finish this book and absorb the information I am giving you, and whether or not you use it, is totally up to you. I cannot force you to do anything. You have the strength within you, as we all do. You just need to dig inside of your mind and find it. Your life; your choice!

How about another test?

All organic things contain what element?

1. Calcium
2. Carbon
3. Chlorophyll

Answer on page 86

Which alcohol can you safely drink?

1. Methanol
2. Ethanol
3. Propanol

Answer on page 89

Which variety of vegetable grows better in a

warmer climate?

   1. Squash
   2. Lettuce
   3. Beet

Answer on page 93

What insect is important in pollination?

   1. Cricket
   2. Termite
   3. Bee

Answer on page 96

I hope you did better this time. If so, then good job!

Pacu fish (cousin of piranhha)

Catfish, but not big enough (a throw-back)

Chapter 15
Typing, Bookkeeping and English

Probably one of the most important classes I took in school, outside of math and science, was typing. I took typing in high school, because that is where the girls were. Also, I took bookkeeping for the same reason. I took the classes for the girls, but as it turned out, these classes became much more important for other reasons. Good typing skills became much more important, because computers have become a way of life for most people. While good typing skills are not mandatory to operate a computer, it does speed things up significantly. I do not know what I would do without a computer. I took my first computer class in college, when computers were the size of cars. Our small local college didn't even have a computer. The programs I had to learn to write in class were sent off to a larger college to run the programs. I did learn to write computer programs to some extent, but that was not as important as the fact I became comfortable using a computer.

I did not use a computer for many years when I got out of school. There was not a great need for a computer in the commercial fishing business. When I started my contracting business, I had the need for a computer again. My new computer was not very user friendly, and the dot matrix printer was poor. The computer was adequate for my business needs, but was not used for anything outside of business. When Windows 95 came out, I upgraded my computer. The new computer was user friendly, smaller and less expensive. I liked the new Windows 95 format, and began using the computer for more than business purposes. As computers continued to do more, come with more memory, and became less expensive, computer uses greatly expanded and have become more accessible to everyone. These days, computers can do most anything, and have become an essential tool for everyone. If you do not know how to use a computer, I suggest you get one and learn how to use it. Once you learn to turn it on, you will be well on your way to learning how to use a computer. Today computers are not hard to learn to use, you just use the pointer (cursor) to navigate through the programs, and click or double click on the features you want to use. When you get into a program, you should be able to quickly navigate through all the tools in the program, and learn rather quickly how to use it. Some programs are easy to use, and some of the more difficult programs may take a little longer to learn, but with the computers these days, you should be able to learn how to use one without outside help. If not, don't be afraid to ask for help. Learning to type will certainly help you write more quickly, but even if you don't know how to type, you should be able to do what you need to do, just a little more slowly. If you get into using the computer, it would be a good idea to take a typing class to learn the proper placement of your hands on the keyboard, and learn where the letters and symbols are located on the keyboard. Or if you prefer, get someone to show you the proper placement of your hands on the computer, then practice, practice, practice. It will take a little practice to learn the keyboard and become efficient at typing, but the skill is well worth the effort.

Bookkeeping, while important, is not so important with today's computers. The bookkeeping class really helped me learn to manage my finances, but these days, the computer bookkeeping programs do most of the work for you, and you really don't need to know a lot about bookkeeping to manage your money, or run a small business. There are programs to help you pay your taxes, manage your checkbook, or manage small business finances with very little actual knowledge of bookkeeping. The key is learning to use the computer itself, and just getting into the programs you need, and learning them basically by trial and error. That is how I learned to use the computer and its programs for the most part, and it worked well for me. I am confident I can do just about anything I need to do with a computer, and most of the programs have similar navigation. Be confident, and just do it. You will learn over time, and I think you will be surprised how fast and easy it is to learn to use a computer. Learning to use a computer can be quite a bit of fun. By trial and error, you will learn to use just what you need, and you will remember from your mistakes. I also suggest you learn one very important thing with computers, and this is to back up your work. Computers are prone to failure, and if you do not back up your work, sooner or later you will lose some of your important work. It is fast and easy to back up the work. Do this every time before you cut off your computer. Also, when working in a program, learn to save your progress as you proceed with what you are doing. You can hit a key and accidentally erase what you are doing. If you do not save at regular intervals, you can easily lose a big portion of what you have done. Computers can also crash, freeze up, or just fail completely at any time, so back up your work. I save my progress on this book every few minutes. Don't underestimate the importance of saving your work often.

English is the language of the majority in the US. If you don't have good English skills, you will be left behind, and you will have a tough time succeeding in the US, to any great extent. You need to be able to converse with the majority of the people here. Yes, there are some areas here and there, where English is not the language of the majority, for example border towns in Texas and California, and China Town in many cities. These are poor areas for the most part. You will not be able to get out of these poor areas to enjoy the greater successes out of your neighborhood, without good English skills. I will not teach you English. Get yourself an English book and study, and talk to your friends and relatives in English. If they do not know English, or have broken English, then learn together. If needed, ask for help. There are classes that will help you gain a working knowledge of the English language. You can get help, and you can learn English. You will be better off for it. Just do it!

If I were going to live in another country, I would learn the language. I spent a lot of time in Ukraine, so I studied and did learn a bit of Russian, not because I had to, but because I wanted to. I felt I should learn the language of the country, so I could function there a little better. Russian is one of the harder languages to learn. They have a completely different alphabet from ours. Not only did I need to learn the language, I needed to learn to read the new symbols they use for letters, and how to pronounce them, along with a couple of accent marks they also use. Again, you are in this country; learn the language. Do it!

And another thing, if you want to come to this country legally and be an American, don't come here and insist on remaining a foreigner. Being an American is learning to speak English. Don't expect to change us to suit you; you are expected to change and Americanize. Don't start your own little country here, as some have already done. I have no problem with legal visitors and welcome legal visitors, and it is OK to act here as you would in your country legally if you are visiting, but if you want to live here permanently, Americanize quickly.

This country is overloaded with illegal invaders, and if you are one of them, it is time to send you home, or put you in a body bag. I have learned to be more tolerant of others due to my aging, but there are a few things I have no tolerance for. I have no tolerance for liars, thieves, hypocrites and illegal invaders. I have no problem with immigrants who want to come here to work, but <u>only</u> if they do so legally. If you only want to come here illegally, and to rape this land, I want you to either go home, or die. If you won't go home, then die! A law we have, which says anyone who is born on American soil, automatically becomes an American, should immediately be eliminated. Only two legal Americans should have American babies, and this should be true regardless of which country the baby is born. This baby would lose its citizenship, if not returned to the US within a year.

Chapter 16
Kingsville and Early Shrimping

After I finished two years at the local college and received my Associate's Degree, I attended a university in Kingsville, which was about 100 miles from home. I stayed in a dormitory, and only went home occasionally. A few of my friends from home also attended the university. I studied pretty hard at first, but as I was becoming frustrated with some of the courses I was taking, I studied less and less and partied more and more. I took a couple semesters of French, because the French teacher was much younger and better looking than the Spanish teacher. A foreign language was required for my curriculum, and it didn't matter which language, so I took French. I tried to do well, but the fact is I didn't do very well at all. I learned a lot of words and phrases, but didn't actually learn to speak French, and I didn't use French when I got out of school, as there was no one to speak French with. I would have been much better off trying to learn Spanish, and wish I had. I would have at least been able to continue my Spanish education with some of the locals back home. Parlez vous Francais?

At a local Saturday night dance sometime in January of 1970, I was drunk as a skunk, whatever that is supposed to mean, just something we said when we were way too drunk, I met the gal who I would later marry. I tried to pick up her sister first, but she wouldn't have anything to do with me. This is not something I remembered, but something I was told later. I was lucky to remember my name the next day. As usual on Saturday night, I had had a little too much Jack Daniels, and couldn't dance very well, but I tried anyway. I would have met this gal and never run across her again, except she had a phone number even a drunk guy could remember, 5555. I called her the next day after I sobered up and got over my hangover, and the rest is history. We married in September of the same year, which was a big mistake as far as the rest of my college life was concerned. My grades were getting worse anyway, but marriage sped up the inevitable process.

I quit school after the fall semester, and in the spring of 1971, moved back home with my bride to a mobile home I had purchased while in school to get out of the school dormitory, which I moved home. I moved the trailer behind my mother and stepdad's home, which was on the river directly across from where I live now. The land I intended to move onto was my dad's. It took some time to prepare to move my trailer there. A well had to be drilled, and the brush had to be cleared first. This is where I became better acquainted with poison ivy, and how to identify it. There was plenty of it, and it itches really badly. When you get a severe case of it, which I did once, and then moderate cases several more times, it makes a lot of little blisters on your skin. You don't even have to touch it, but can also get a good case when you burn the stuff and get into the smoke, which is inevitable. There was so much poison ivy, there was no way I was going to avoid the stuff, and I didn't. Just disturbing the stuff will put their chemicals into the air. I got most of the poison ivy cleared out eventually, and had fewer problem with this nasty vine.

While we were still in the trailer behind my mother and stepdad's, one night there was a terrible thunderstorm with a cold front. The trailer was not blocked or tied down, because we were only there temporarily. That storm blew in at about 70 mph, and I was certain the trailer was going to blow over. It rocked back and forth for several hours, and probably did come very close to blowing over. It would not have gone far, as the trailer was between two big trees, but luckily the trees did not have to keep us from blowing away. It was very scary though.

After several months cleaning up the lot, where we were going to move the trailer, the electrical service got installed, the well dug, and the trailer moved in. It took a while to block the trailer, install the storm anchors and install the water and sewer lines, but I worked day and night, and got it done as quickly as I could. We set up housekeeping, and I began my new career, the family business, fishing and shrimping.

My mother was the daughter of a commercial fisherman, and she developed a need or want, whatever you want to call it, to get into the shrimping business while she was running her bars. She was making plenty of money, and bought a boat mainly to have fun on. This boat was a lot of fun for her, and she had so much fun and made a lot of money on the small boat, she bought another bigger boat. I spent a lot of time on the little boat helping my mother, making some money and learning the business. This little boat would eventually become my first boat. My mother bought a third boat, and later talked my stepdad into building a fourth boat. He was a good builder and welder, and built a very comfortable boat. My stepdad never really liked shrimping, but he never complained and worked hard at the business. He was a hard worker, and I learned to appreciate him for that.

I helped my mother on the small boat, and also worked on one of my brother-in-law's boats at times, through the spring, summer and into the fall. Then, when the shrimping season was over, I fished in the Guadalupe River for catfish through the wintertime. It was hard work, but the money was good. The following year, my wife and I ran my mother's little boat on our own. I even ran the boat alone a few times. Shrimping on my mother's little boat (25 feet long) was quite an experience, and I spent entirely too much time working on the gasoline engine to keep it running, but fortunately it wasn't big enough to venture far from home. I even got into the water once, and pulled it home by the bow rope. I didn't catch a lot of shrimp, but I did learn a lot about working on a gasoline engine, and keeping a shrimp net in one piece. I learned a lot about the shallow areas of the bay near town, where at times there were a lot of shrimp, just not this particular year.

The following year I ran my dad's larger boat (45 feet) with a dependable diesel engine, where I could venture out into the open areas of the bay, and when there was no shrimp locally, I could travel to other bays much easier than I could with the smaller and not very dependable boat I started with. Now begins the really hard work and a wealth of knowledge by doing, but also from a lot of fixing, because something is always breaking or needing attention, but I had plenty of experience doing this from my work on the small boat owned by my mother. I worked as a shrimper up and down the Texas Gulf Coast from Corpus Christi to Cameron, Louisiana. I learned all the bays, and how to catch shrimp. When we ventured away from home, we lived on the boat. The longest stretch my wife and I lived on the boat was six weeks, while working in Galveston one year. My wife and I always worked together during these early years shrimping.

I made a lot of modifications to my dad's boat after running it for a while. Those modifications made the boat easier to run and more comfortable, so I could even run the boat entirely by myself, which I also did a little later. The original cabin on the boat was very small, and I ended up cutting it off and completely rebuilt a new cabin that was much larger and more comfortable. The new cabin was large enough for a couch that folded out into a bed, a cook stove with sink and cabinets to store food, and a water tank on the top of the cabin to hold water for the shower I installed below the deck. It had two large comfortable pedestal chairs in the front of the wheelhouse. This was important, as we would spend sometimes days and even weeks on the boat. I installed windows all the way around the cabin for good visibility, and the boat was very comfortable and big enough for me and my wife, who ran the boat with me, and after five years of marriage, the first of three kids. My youngest daughter spent the most time on the boat of our three kids, five years, until she started school. She was even on the boat the day before she was born. My son spent only two years on the boat until the oldest started school, and the youngest daughter spent very little time on the boat, as by the time she came along, the shrimping business was going down the tubes to oblivion.

Shrimping is a business that is always up and down from year to year, and even when shrimping was good, you could not always depend on shrimping alone to earn a living, so I worked with and for one of my brother-in-laws many times. He could run his boat in the bays easily alone, but when it was necessary to venture into the Gulf of Mexico to make a few bucks, he didn't dare go alone for safety reasons, and he was always in need of a deckhand. I was often that deckhand. I learned a lot about sharks out there with him. The biggest shark we caught was only seven feet long, but we caught many. We would rather have not caught any though, as they were taking money from us by biting holes in our net. A shark liver tied to the sack of the net acted as a deterrent to other sharks, but that was in addition to shark gear which covered the tail end, the sack, of the net. We never completely avoided problems with sharks though.

We worked as pipe insulators at the South Texas Nuclear Project one year, when it was getting built. My brother-in-law knew how to insulate pipe, and use the tools of the trade. I was his helper, so I learned to insulate pipe. Not a trade I would really care to go into for any length of time, but when shrimping was bad, we did whatever was available to make ends meet. I also learned to dredge oysters with my brother-in-law on his boat. Oysters grow on reefs mostly and are dredged with an iron frame dredge. I say they grow mostly on reefs, because they also grow singly scattered in some areas and single oysters can be very good. These are dredged with a lighter basket dredge, because of the soft mud you are dredging in. The heavier dredges would dig too deep into the soft mud bottom. My brother-in-law and I only dredged oysters around reefs. We spent all day going around and around in a circle on the edges of reefs containing live oysters, and periodically pulled up and dumped the dredge on a table on the deck of the boat. We then culled the oysters while the dredge was dredging up more oysters. The oysters are picked out and broken apart, as they often come up in clusters of several oysters, and thrown onto the deck into a pile. This is very tough work. When you have a big pile of oysters, they are shoveled into sacks after being measured with a bushel basket. Oysters are sold by the bushel, which is approximately 120 pounds. Handling these sacks is a chore in itself. The worst thing about dredging for oysters was generally the weather. This was done during the winter time when it was cold and nasty outside. Usually the best oysters to be had were in January and February, though the season opened in November. At times my brother-in-law and I also worked for the oyster houses opening oysters. There was not much money in opening oysters, but it was money nevertheless.

Everyone in the family liked to play card games, and we did this for recreation quite often. We played poker and pinochle most of the time, but we played dominos too—straight dominos, moon, and forty-two. We never played for big stakes, only friendly family games, often playing for pennies. This was just a way to relax. As hard as we worked, we needed time to relax often. There were times we played until the early morning hours.

There were several years when we were doing well with shrimping and fishing, we were able to take several hunting vacations with my in-laws to New Mexico to hunt mule deer. I seldom hunted for trophies. I hunted for meat around home, though there were some deer I killed, that were at least trophies for me. But I was hunting for a trophy mule deer when we went on these hunts to New Mexico. The trips were good vacations for the family as well. The first two years we went, we didn't kill any deer, but had a lot of fun playing in the mountains. We enjoyed the mountains, and the trips down the mountain, to White Sands near Alamogordo, NM. I learned to drive in snow, and how to use tire chains. I learned what my truck could and could not do. Driving in snow is not so hard, but ice is a whole new ballgame. You cannot drive on ice, period. Well, maybe with tires made for driving on ice, but we didn't have any.

The second two years we went to New Mexico, I killed, first a small buck, and then a trophy buck. The first little buck was larger than the whitetail bucks we hunted in Texas. We were driving along a trail on the ridge of a mountain range, when I saw the little buck running toward us. A red jeep was following the buck, but they didn't see the deer. Knowing some of the traits of mule deer enabled me to kill this buck. There was a brush line, off about 50 feet, on each side of the road on which we were driving. I knew the buck would go into this brush when he got a little closer to me and saw my truck. I turned and parked my truck, then waited for the buck, with my gun ready. When the buck got closer to me, he angled toward the brush line, and I knew he would stop and look back at the red jeep. Mule deer, unlike whitetail deer, will not rush headlong into brush. The little buck ran right up to the brush line and suddenly stopped. He looked back at the red jeep. That is when I shot him in the heart. He jumped straight up and fell to the ground, dead from the heart shot.

The next year on the last day of the season, I came across a trophy buck. Knowing another trait of mule deer enabled me to kill this one. If a mule deer thinks it is hid well, it will not move until you go by. When I spotted the deer, he was in heavy brush. All I could see was his black nose and eyes shining. I looked at him in the scope on my rifle, and could then see the base of the antlers. I could not tell how big the antlers were, but could tell from the size of their bases, it was larger than the one from the previous year. I set my crosshairs on its throat and pulled the trigger. This deer was big and very heavy. My wife and I had a really difficult time getting him into the back of the truck.

The next day it was time to go home. The in-laws had left that morning. We put the deer on the front of my father-in-law's jeep we pulled with our truck, and headed home. It was nearly dark by the time we got going. My wife, her younger sister, and the two kiddos we had at the time, left our cabin in the mountains. It had already started snowing, and we had not gone fifteen miles, when the snow got too thick on the road to go further pulling the jeep. I had to unhook the jeep, get the deer off the front of the jeep and put it in the rear, so my wife and sister-in-law could drive the jeep out of the mountains separately. I had no gloves handy. I learned about frostbite, and it is very painful when your hands thaw out. Though my frostbite was not severe, it was very painful. I also learned how to drive out of the mountains in a blizzard without four-wheel drive. That was no fun, and in hindsight I would never do it again.

Though the two mule deer were trophies for me, I learned the quality of the meat from the two deer was much better than whitetail deer we hunted back home. There is no comparison between the two. Mule deer are better, hands down. And the mule deer were much larger. The trophy buck was over 200 pounds.

Years later, I went a couple more times, first with my son and nephew, and then again, with my son and daughter-in-law. My son killed a buck on the second trip. The first year with my son and nephew, a mountain lion stalked my son and me close to dark, when we were trying to get back to our truck. My son didn't want me to kill the lion, so I shot at it to scare it. It didn't scare. We took another route to our truck in a different direction. We didn't see the lion again. My nephew told us, when we later met at the truck, a mountain lion charged another hunter. The other hunter managed to shoot the lion before it got him.

Chapter 17
Shrimping

Shrimp are migratory little creatures, and there are several kinds of shrimp. Different varieties of shrimp move in and out of the coastal bays, over the course of the year. For the most part, we chased brown shrimp in the bays during the summer and white shrimp in the fall. Brown shrimp season starts on May 15th and lasts for two months. Then there is a break for a month, after which white shrimp season opens on August 15th and lasts for four months, though the shrimp usually only lasted a couple months, or sometimes as many as three months. It depended upon how early the cold fronts cooled the water, which would drive the shrimp to the warmer waters of the Gulf of Mexico. White shrimp, which we also called green tails, have a little bright green color on their tails. Brown shrimp have reddish-brown color on their tails.

Shrimp migrate from the Gulf of Mexico into the bays as young shrimp, and grow up in the bays. As they grow larger, they migrate back to the saltier waters of the Gulf of Mexico. Shrimp also migrate up and down the coast of the Gulf of Mexico. Some years there will be more shrimp in one or two of the bays, than there will be in others. This may be partly due to the amount of rainfall up and down the coast, as the tiny shrimp, and the white shrimp in particular, need freshwater to grow well. In years where there is plenty of rainfall, there will usually be more white shrimp, but often they will be smaller due to their greater abundance and the fight for food and space. A single adult white shrimp can produce a million young.

Brown shrimp prefer a little saltier water than do white shrimp, and the brown shrimp are not as dependent upon freshwater as are white shrimp. Years where there is limited rainfall, brown shrimp will be more plentiful in the bays, as too much rainfall will keep them farther out in the bays, nearer the Gulf of Mexico, and they would leave the bay before the season was over. Some species do not migrate into the bays, as they need little or no freshwater. These are rock shrimp, pink shrimp and seabobs. There is another shrimp called a cotton shrimp, but no one I ever talked to, knew whether it was a sick shrimp or a species of its own. It resembled a white shrimp, and the only apparent difference was the meat of the shrimp was cotton white, instead of the semi-transparent norm of the white shrimp. It was always found with white shrimp, but I cannot tell you whether it was actually a white shrimp, or another species.

There is another brown shrimp called a hopper, we sometimes caught in the spring, and these shrimp were a little more elusive. We had to catch them at night, and this was usually in March and April. There was no season for this minor shrimp species. Hoppers have a small black spot on each side of the body, and are a little more reddish maroon than the brown shrimp. Brown shrimp and hoppers seem to be closely related and are very similar in appearance, with a characteristic groove on each side of their horn on their head. The white shrimp have no such groove, and have much longer whiskers. As we had to shrimp for hoppers at night, we had to know the waters in which we were shrimping very well; every reef, every piling, the inter-coastal waterway and oil and gas well platforms that were in the bay. Some things had lights on them, so you could see them at night, and some things didn't.

Navigation was also very difficult at times, due to fog during the spring and fall. Most of the time, we had only one 100-watt bulb at the top of the mast on the boat to light the way, except when we were culling the shrimp, when we had 200 watts in the deck lights, so we could see to cull the shrimp. We had a high power spotlight we could use to light the way when we were traveling, or just needed to see something a little better out the front of the boat, but usually the mast light was sufficient. There were also running lights on the boat, a small red light on the port side of the cabin, a small green light on the starboard side of the cabin, and a white light in the middle. These running lights do not put out enough light for navigation, but are used so other boats can tell which direction you are headed from a distance by the color of the lights visible from where they are. The left side of the boat is the port side, the right side the starboard side, and the front of the boat is the bow and the rear is the stern. An easy way to remember the sides of the boat is by the length of the words. Left, port, and red go together, while right, starboard, and green go together.

A little piece of knowledge I learned while shrimping at night, was every night the moon would come up a little earlier. Early in the moon cycle, it would already be up and well onto setting in the west, and be only a sliver of moon, when we got out on the water after the sun went down. Each successive night, the visible moon would be a little bigger and higher in the sky, and we would get a little more moonlight. Finally, by the time the moon was full, the moon would be up most of the night, and we could see fairly well without our mast light though this light was always on. When there was no moon or only half a moon, much of the night was worked with little natural light.

When you cull shrimp, you see all the little critters living in the bays besides just shrimp. There were always a lot of croaker, hardheads (saltwater catfish), gafftop (another species of saltwater catfish), plenty of small shad, and of course crabs. A little fact about hardheads and gafftop is the male of these two species carry their young, in the form of eggs, in their mouth until the babies grow to the point they can swim on their own. We caught flounder, squid, small trout, and jelly, some of which was pretty hot because of the chemicals in the jelly. Sometimes we would take the flounder and squid home to eat. Squid, or calamari, was not such a delicacy as it is today, but we ate them regularly. Many jellies were also bioluminescent. When driving the boat at night, these jellies would light up in the water behind the boat, when the jelly was disturbed by the boat's propeller. Some jellyfish have long tentacles and they contain poison that will burn your skin. Getting these poisons on us was an everyday affair when there was jelly around, which was most of the time. After the jelly was in the net for a while, much of the poison would wash out of them and the stings were not as severe, but sufficient to be noticeable.

Then there are some not so common critters, such as dog fish, an occasional octopus, and ribbon fish which look like flat silver snakes. Ribbon fish have sharp teeth similar to a snake's fangs. There were piggy perch, brittle stars that were very delicate and would break when you touch them, and different varieties of crabs other than the common blue crab. There were spider crabs, stone crabs, and so many more varieties I could not begin to name them all. Take my word for it; there are really a lot of different kinds of crabs. The large pincer of the stone crab is edible, but I don't really care for its taste as much as I do some other crabs, such as blue crab and king crab, my favorite from Alaska. Only one pincer of the stone crab can be harvested legally, as removing both pincers would leave it unable to feed itself, and it would die. The body of the crab is small and inedible. You can bend a crab's claw, and when under sufficient strain and pain I'm sure, the crab will let go of the pincer without hurting the crab significantly. The crab will then grow a new pincer.

Most people have heard of a sanddollar, but few have ever seen a live one. They are usually found on the beach and are dead, smooth and white after being bleached out by the sun. Live sanddollars are greenish and have tiny spines all over them. Inside a sanddollar are tiny bones shaped like little white birds (dove, some say). Sanddollars are quite numerous off the coast of Texas in the Gulf of Mexico, and at times we caught them by the thousands in our net.

There is a variety of jellyfish call the cabbage head, or cannonball, as we called them, because they are round like a cannonball. This variety is notable because at times I have seen them so thick they literally covered the surface of the water for miles. These cannonballs were a problem, because they settled to the bottom of the water during the night, and you might start shrimping in the early morning, which is when we almost always started, and not see the cannonballs, but they were there. You could literally fill your net with these cannonballs in a matter of a couple minutes, maybe 10,000 pounds of these very heavy little creatures. All you could do is dump your net and everything in it and start over. As the sun got up in the morning, the cannonballs would come to the surface and not cause any problems, as long as you didn't get into too shallow water.

A shrimp net only catches things a few feet off the bottom of the water. If you are in four feet of water, you can catch pretty much everything in the water. In maybe ten feet of water, you do not catch anything in the upper area of the water over about four feet. We later learned to use a bib on our nets, to catch shrimp farther up in the water column, as shrimp are not always only on the bottom. We were always finding new ways to catch more shrimp. I invented the cutback net, which made a legal 32-foot net, out of a 64-foot net. This worked very well for a while, but the TP&WD changed the regulations to make the cutback net illegal. The cutback net enabled me and many other shrimpers to catch more shrimp for a couple years as the invention caught on.

You had to be a pretty good weatherman to be a shrimper. Weather can be very dangerous, and I've been caught in a few storms I wasn't prepared for. If I had had my choice, I would have been home instead of out on the water. The storms were not damaging, but very scary. Lightning struck my boat once, and turned the fiberglass antennas on the boat to splinters. The lightning also melted the inside of the radios and destroyed them. It was just lucky a fire wasn't started, as this happened one night when I was not on the boat. Water spouts are fairly common on the water, and I have seen my fair share. These aren't quite as large or dangerous as a land tornado, but if they hit your boat, they can cause plenty of damage. As I said, I have seen quite a few of these, but never came all that close to getting hurt by one. I did see three in the bay at one time around me once, and that was a little scary, but even though they were all within a half mile of me, they caused no damage to me or my boat. When clouds turn green, they contain hail, and if they are severe enough to contain hail, they are big enough to produce a tornado or water spout. Funnels hanging out of clouds were a very common occurrence while we were shrimping, but most of these tails never produced a waterspout. I recall counting thirteen tails hanging out of a long cloud across the horizon early one morning while heading out shrimping. As the sun came up, these tails dissipated, and it turned out to be a very productive day at work.

Shrimp size is measured by the number of shrimp per pound. When we sold our shrimp to fish houses, a five-pound sample of shrimp was counted and the number of shrimp in this sample divided by five, to give you the average count of shrimp per pound. This was used to determine the price we were paid for the shrimp. Shrimp are categorized by count brackets. Some of the brackets are 26-30's, 21-25's, and 19-21's and this means there are say between 26 and 30 shrimp per pound of shrimp in the 26-30 shrimp bracket. Each bracket will have a different price and the smaller the number, the bigger the shrimp and usually the higher the price. The biggest shrimp I have caught were 3-5's. These were very large shrimp. It is quite rare for shrimp to average this large. 21-25's to 36-40's is common from year to year for white shrimp in the bays, and 40-50's to 80-100's is common for the brown bait shrimp during the May to June summer season in the bays. All species would grow larger when they matured in the Gulf of Mexico, than the ones we caught shrimping in the coastal bays. White shrimp can live about five years if they are lucky, and can grow as large as around six ounces each. Though bigger shrimp will usually be found in the Gulf of Mexico, we did not venture into the Gulf much, because of the size of our boat, though we did from time to time, when there were not many shrimp to catch in the coastal bays.

Shrimp have a lot of iodine in them, and even more so when

they mature. This affects their taste and we always liked and ate the shrimp we caught in the bays, more than the ones we caught in the Gulf, due to a lesser amount of iodine in the shrimp from the bays. We often headed the shrimp we caught, especially when shrimping in the Gulf, or when we took shrimp home to put in the freezer. You could feel the iodine burning your fingers while heading the shrimp. It is also possible to get iodine poisoning from heading these shrimp, and I have known a person or two to whom this has happened. While I could feel the iodine burn many times while heading shrimp, I never got iodine poisoning.

    I remember one time we were shrimping in the Gulf of Mexico off of Galveston, and were catching some very large shrimp, but we had to go way out to get them. The weather was calm most of the time. We had ventured about 50 miles from Galveston, and were making five day trips to conserve fuel, and allow us enough time to make a decent catch. We had made several trips, and the weather was perfect every trip, so my dad decided he wanted to come along, and came up to Galveston. My dad was not very salty, as he never spent any time in the open waters of the Gulf of Mexico, but he did like the water. After about the second day of our trip, we were catching shrimp in decent amounts, and the weather again was perfect. Then late in the evening, the wind came up and our anchor would not hold so we could sleep. We had to make our way to an oil well platform to tie up to, but it was pitch black and by the time we got started good, the waves were ten feet high and the boat was really bouncing up and down. We were in no real danger, but we needed to tie up to the well to get some sleep. It took us until midnight to get to the well, and we got tied up after we chased the sea birds away. My not so salty dad swallowed his chewing tobacco while he was trying to put the bow rope on the well, and he ended up getting a little sea sick. The next morning everything was calm again, and after another day shrimping we went back to Galveston to unload our catch. My dad never asked to go back out into the Gulf of Mexico again. I think he enjoyed the trip mostly, but he had had enough of the rough water, and gained a little more respect for what I did, and the toughness I have gained through shrimping. Maybe you will appreciate the shrimp you eat a little more too, the next time you do so.

After unloading my shrimp and my dad, we loaded up with fuel and ice and headed back out into the Gulf, where we had been catching shrimp for several weeks. The first morning back at our job, we saw a big gulf boat several miles offshore from us. I got on the CB radio to see if I could find the captain of this boat talking to anyone. I finally found him on one of the channels. He wasn't saying much, just talking to a buddy in the distance somewhere. I continued to monitor this boat on the radio. Late in the evening, I heard him say he saw a boat on the beach, and that that boat, me, was there all day. He said he was going to check me out in the morning. The next morning, I was again at my shrimping spot and catching shrimp. This big gulf boat was there too, making a few drags. I heard him tell his buddy there were some shrimp here, and this one boat continued to shrimp in our area the remainder of the day. The next morning there were fifty boats there, each dragging two nets, and they wiped out my shrimping spot. That was the last day I worked this area. It just didn't seem fair, but no one ever said life was fair, right? Remember that.

Shrimping is a seven day a week job when the season is open. The weather does not generally deter us from making our living, but from time to time, it has been really rough. Once again, while shrimping in Galveston Bay, I remember I shrimped until noon, when a hurricane was coming in. I unloaded my catch, which was really good just before the storm, and then raced across the bay into a river for protection from the storm, if you can call ten mph racing, as that was the top speed of the boat. The storm did come in later that evening, and after a long night on the boat, I woke up with brush all over the boat from broken tree limbs, due to the high winds. Other than the brush on the boat, there was no damage. I went back across the bay to load up with ice and fuel, and got back to the chore at hand, making a living on the elusive little crustacean—shrimp.

We pulled one main net on our boat and a try net. The main net for the May 15th summer season had a maximum spread of thirty-two feet by law. There was no limit on the spread of the net during the August 15th fall season, and we pulled a net with a sixty- five foot spread. The try net usually had about a seven foot spread, and we would pull this net for a few minutes at a time, to test the amount of shrimp on the bottom in the area. If there were not enough shrimp in the try net, we ventured on until we could find sufficient shrimp. The try net was not very big and was quickly lowered and raised, so we could test several areas for shrimp. We used a CB radio to talk to friends and family who were shrimping in the area. This helped determine where the best shrimping was. We would help each other so we could all catch some shrimp and make a living. When we found sufficient shrimp, the big net was lowered into the water and the harvest began. We would still continue to pull the try net at regular intervals to test the water for shrimp, and insure we were making money. The largest haul of shrimp I made in my career during a two-hour drag was just over a thousand pounds. The most shrimp I caught dollar wise in a single day was just over $5,000.00. That was a very good day.

A little trick I learned with the try net from my brother-in-law was to tie a small twine that was not stretchy, usually a polyester thread about the size of a small fishing line, to the top of the try net. The twine was run to a fishing reel on the boat. The try net was lowered to the bottom and the small twine would spool off the reel, then I could grab the string and hold onto the string with a finger, and feel the little bumps when shrimp would jump into the try net and hit the top of the net where the string was tied. The more shrimp I could feel hitting the top of the little net, the more shrimp we were catching in the big net. Shrimp school up and sometimes get pretty thick. When I would feel a lot of shrimp hitting the top of the try net, I would circle the boat and drag the net in the same area for a while to catch more shrimp. The thump string, as it was called, gave a real time measurement of the shrimp we were catching. Sometimes I could feel fish hitting the net, so I had to pull the try net, though not as frequently, to verify what I was feeling was actually shrimp. The thump string accomplished the same thing as constantly raising and lowering the try net, but gave me real time measurements, and lowered the amount of work necessary to measure what we were catching. This worked very well most of the time. The thump string did not work in the deeper waters of the Gulf of Mexico, as the length of string necessary was too long, and you could not feel the tiny bumps the shrimp would make. The thump string only worked well in shallow waters up to about eight feet deep. Our boat drew two and a half feet of water, and we worked very well in waters of three feet or more. Occasionally, we would drag bottom a little as shrimp had no boundaries, and often got thick in shallow waters.

Running a shrimp boat means learning many, many tasks to keep it in good running order. No one is going to tell you what you have to do and what you don't have to do, but if you don't do what is required to keep the boat in good order, you will pay a hefty price in equipment failures eventually. This can cost you a lot of money, not just in repairs, but also in lost revenue from downtime, so you had to keep up the maintenance. This was just part of being responsible. You doing the things you should be doing are no different, regardless of your job. If you have no job, maybe you didn't do your maintenance. Maintenance is a part of life and when you are young, you probably have your parents making certain you do what is required of you. If not, then you have to grow up pretty quickly. If you do not take care of the maintenance, then you will never grow up, though you may appear to be grown. Maintenance may have been neglected when you should have been studying in school, or learning a new task at your current job, or taking a night class to learn a new trade or skill. Lack of maintenance is probably why you are in such a pickle now. If you have been a slacker, then you are going to pay the price now, if you ever expect to get out of your rut. Be responsible.

To be a shrimper, you have to know how to maintain the diesel motor by changing oil and filters, changing the fuel filters, repairing copper lines, keeping things greased that need greasing, keeping the drive train to the winch in good order and occasionally making repairs, usually by welding, which is another trade I learned reasonably well. We usually hauled the boat completely out of the water around the first of August, to clean the bottom of barnacles and repaint the bottom and sides, so I was a painter too. The bottom was painted with a copper paint into which we also added a can of red pepper to deter growth of algae and barnacles. The sides were painted with epoxy (two-part) paint, which is more durable than ordinary paint. There are all sorts of boat rigging that need constant repair and replacement, such as the whip line used to bring in the net, the double block and tackle used to lift the sack of the shrimp net with shrimp, crabs, fish, and whatever onto the boat for culling. During the day we usually only pulled the tail end (the sack), of the net in with a lazy line to dump our catch. This took only about ten minutes. The lazy line is a rope used to pull the sack to the side of the boat. We only brought in the entire net when there was a problem with the net, or we were going home for the evening. Of course, the net always needed attention when there became holes in the net. These repairs were often made on the trip home. Porpoise would bite holes in the webbing, as they followed the net. They would bite small fish out of the net and take some webbing with the fish. Sharks would also bite holes in the net. This was not such a problem when in the bays, but when in the Gulf, sharks became a major problem. Normal wear and tear on the net also caused holes. Sandy bottom is abrasive, and eventually caused holes. Dragging too close to an oyster reef, the sharp edges of the oysters would cut and wear on the net. Even when not close to a reef, there was sometimes scattered shell. Then there were snags here and there, and would tear the hell out of a net, resulting in a major repair job. Major net repairs were always time consuming. I spent a lot of time repairing my nets.

Patching a net hole is time consuming and not always that easy, as there is a particular method in repairing a net to match the existing webbing, especially if these holes are quite large. This is not easy to do, not easy to teach, and takes a lot of practice and patience. You can just lace up a hole, but over time as you tear more holes in the net and continue to just lace up the holes, this will pull the webbing enough to affect the working ability of the entire net. Patching by lacing the hole up can be done for a temporary repair, but later the net will need to be repaired correctly.

Oyster dredges worked the bays, dredging up dead shell used to build roads. Barges and barges of dead shell were dredged from our local bay. Tow boats were constantly pushing these barges across the bay. There were drilling companies, drilling oil and gas wells, and all the boats servicing these rigs and wells. All this activity in the bays resulted in lost buckets, lost car tires used for bumpers on most boats, and pieces of wire cable, 55 gallon drums and other junk we would inevitably catch in our nets. This junk really caused a mess with our shrimp haul and tore up our nets. These were some of the many hazards to shrimping, and there was nothing we could do, but clean up the mess and try to salvage our shrimp, repair our nets and keep on working. The oyster dredges would churn up mud around the dredges, and shrimp seemed to like this soft freshly dredged up mud, therefore we tended to shrimp around these dredges. Though they marked the holes they were dredging, at times we tended to get a little too close to this soft mud and holes, and paid the price with muddy shrimp that had to be cleaned really thoroughly before selling. Occasionally, we even bogged our nets in one of these holes.

The peeling on shrimp does not grow with the creature; therefore, shrimp need to shed their skin from time to time as they grow. The same is true for crabs. They would bury in the sand or mud to protect themselves from predators when they are soft after peeling, and the soft mud from the dredges made it easier for them to bury up, which is maybe one reason they liked the soft mud. Mussels were also chewed up by the dredging process, and this would provide a lot of food (meat from the mussel), and a source of calcium (shell from the mussel), for the soft shrimp which could not get around very well, and had a difficult time searching for food on its own. We would catch crabs occasionally that had shed their hard shells, and this was a real treat, as we could clean the crabs and cook them with the legs and pincers attached and eat the whole crab.

A major requirement for a shrimper was learning to tie knots which would hold, and with ropes that were always in reasonably good condition. A rope break or knot failure could cause your boat to get away from you while tied up. A rope failure can also cause more work and even hurt you. There are many other details all shrimpers must learn, from attaching the net to the doors, which spread the net open, to adjusting the jump chain, which makes shrimp jump off the bottom and go inside the net when it is pulled. The net is pulled at about two miles per hour behind the boat, with cables running from the doors to the winch on the boat. You need to keep the net out of the wheel wash from the propeller of the boat as much as you can, as this will scatter the shrimp in shallow water and decrease your catch.

A normal drag of the net was one and a half to two hours, after which time the net was brought up, the boat tied in a circle, the tail end of the net brought up with the lazy line, and the block and tackle attached to the sack of the net. The sack was lifted onto the boat and the catch dumped onto the deck. The net was then put back over and another drag started, while we culled shrimp on deck out of the fish, crabs, jelly, and other junk. We then washed the shrimp, and iced them down in an ice box with crushed ice. This process was repeated five or six times during the day, and occasionally more. A normal day during the fall white shrimp season, was easily fourteen plus hours. Up at 4:00 AM and you were lucky to get into bed by 10:00 PM. This is why we stayed on the boat often, to get some sleep. Trash was scooped back overboard and the sea gulls, terns, and pelicans had a field day eating the byproduct of the catch. Porpoise also followed the boats much of the time, and also had their fill.

Shrimping in the local bays and the Gulf of Mexico is a really good education, and while a great deal of work and long hours, quite fulfilling. There are so many critters and sights to see, most people never get the chance to see. The beauty of brittle starfish, schools of mullet running for miles on top of the water, shark and jack fish that follow the boat. There are different kinds of jelly including man-of-war that will sting you badly, cabbage heads, pancake jelly which is a pale pink and about a foot in diameter and a couple inches thick, and comb jelly which is small and not very dangerous and has ribs resembling comb teeth. Then there is the common white jellyfish, with long strings of tentacles that can cause severe burns on the skin. There are manta rays and stingrays, and I have seen manta rays up to ten feet across milling around feeding on the top of the water in the Gulf of Mexico. A strange and semi-dangerous little creature we called a sea louse, but correctly known as a mantis shrimp, resembled a shrimp and has four horns on its tail. When picked up, it would try to stick these horns into your fingers. There were always plenty of hermit crabs in the shallow waters, and the speedy fiddler crabs that would scurry around on the beach.

All the wonderful creatures to see living in, on and around the water were always entertaining, but probably the best thing about shrimping is that you get away from people. You get out into nature and do your own thing with very few people around. You feel very free when you are out on the water, and see maybe one or two boats in the distance, and there is no one to bother you. You also have a lot of time to think about a lot of things. People really need time to think about their life, their future and the things they need to do to make their lives better. In the hustle and bustle of life, many people do not have this time to think, and in the long term this hurts their lives. Do you have think time?

There were times when the boats would get pretty thick, especially at the opening of a new season, but as the season wore on and the shrimp became scarcer, the boats would spread out and there was peace on the water. You could hear the wind and the waves and a few birds, but there was very little noise outside of the hum of the engine to shatter your peaceful day. Much is the same when you go camping or go into the mountains to get away from it all. This was an everyday occurrence much of the time while shrimping, and especially true when shrimping in the Gulf of Mexico. When we were shrimping 50 miles from Galveston in the Gulf, we would go days and not even see a boat. Peace!

When you spend a lot of time on the water away from civilization and specifically doctors, you had to be a good doctor yourself. I always had cuts, burns and punctures, and had to be able to deal with these to avoid infection. I learned to doctor myself well enough and seldom go to the doctor, but just as important is to know when you really do need professional help. I don't use many medications, mainly ibuprofen, hemorrhoid ointment, triple antibiotic, and Clorox makes good bacterial disinfectant, but when it comes to pneumonia and strep throat, I have visited the doctor. I have also had several sebaceous cysts on my back, that had to be cut out, and once I had a shrimp horn in a finger I couldn't get out. Shrimp have a needle sharp horn sticking out of the front of their head, and we always got stuck here and there when culling the shrimp and de-heading the shrimp. They were not nearly as bad though, as the baby saltwater catfish horns that got me often and were really painful. Catfish have one dorsal (back) fin and two lateral (side) fins behind their head, and there is also a serrated bony horn on the front side of these fins. I have been stuck by the baby catfish, maybe three or four inches long, with horns a quarter inch long, while culling my shrimp haul, and have stuck these horns all the way into my fingers many times. Sometimes three or four times a day. They are extremely painful and poisonous, so you have to squeeze the blood out for a few seconds once you pull the horn out, so your fingers don't get sore from the poison. Sometimes I would squirt the blood several feet, but this was good because it was washing the poison out of my finger. It gives me chills now to think about that. Anyway, back to the shrimp horn, I got one in the end of a finger very deeply and it broke off. I tried for weeks to get it out with a needle, and thought I did a time or two as it would heal over, but it would never heal inside. I finally decided I couldn't get it out and had a doctor burn the thing out. I watched him with his little electric arc burning tool, and he burned a hole all the way down to the bone. Thank goodness for Novocain or whatever he used to numb my finger.

One thing you hear more about these days is red tide. We saw red tide and experienced it up close and personal one year in particular, though we saw it in limited amounts a few other years. I don't remember what year it was, but we were shrimping in Lavaca Bay that year, and the red tide was especially bad. It did not affect the shrimp much at first, and we were allowed to catch the shrimp in this red tide. The biologists said it did not affect the quality of the shrimp. Red tide is a natural occurrence, and is caused by a type of algae in the water, more prevalent in drought years, when there is not enough freshwater flowing into the bays. When these algae bloom it produces a toxin which contaminates the water. When very thick as it was this year, it turned the water nearly brown, and you could smell the toxin. It would burn your eyes a bit. It would also make your allergies flare up, and make you sneeze a lot. Though it did not affect the shrimp much, it did affect the fish. It killed many of the fish and other creatures that couldn't get away from the red tide. When we would pick up our hauls of shrimp, there would be very little culling, as there was nothing in the drag but shrimp. All we had to do was scoop the shrimp into baskets, wash, and ice them down. It made the work very easy, as long as we could find the shrimp. The red tide lasted for months, and it later became difficult to find shrimp. They probably were killed, but hopefully they migrated away from the red tide. There is always something to deal with, and this is just one of the many things we had to deal with as shrimpers.

We had to deal with oyster grass, black seaweed that grows

usually near oyster reefs. Some years it was worse than other years, and there were some areas of the bay where it was more prone to grow. You could not drag your shrimp net in areas where there was a lot of oyster grass for very long, as it would affect the working ability of your net, and after a short while, you would not be catching the shrimp you would be dragging your net through. There was always something that would cling to the net, affecting its working ability after a while. This was not a problem much of the time, but a serious problem at other times. A lot of anything other than shrimp was a problem, and there is a lot of stuff besides shrimp to catch. Some of these include too many fish, too much jelly, too many crabs, muck, slime, sticks, tires, discarded cable, clams, seaweed, and the list goes on and on.

For a while we raised two small dogs on the boat, a male and a female, and the male learned to play with crabs. He would grab a crab out of the pile of fish, shrimp, and crabs when dumped onto the deck of the boat, and carefully removed the pincers one at a time with his teeth. Then he would kill the crab. He was bitten by the crabs numerous times, but over time learned to avoid being bitten. He would almost playfully toss the crabs around, as he expertly removed the pincers. By killing crabs on the boat, he became a natural killer of critters. He wasn't very big, maybe fifteen pounds dripping wet, but he got home and had the need to kill. He always found stuff around the house to kill. He was the gentlest dog around with our kids, but killed snakes, armadillo, opossum, and anything else he could find, with a vengeance. But he wouldn't bother our other pets. In fact, at times we had dogs, cats, chickens, ducks, and once even a pet deer eating out of the same food bowl. Willie was my buddy, my friend and once my savior, when he snatched a cottonmouth from under my feet, and took off slinging the large snake in his mouth, tearing it to pieces.

My wife and I had three kids, first a girl, then a boy and then another girl. We raised the kids on the boat up until the time they got into school, when my wife had to stay home, take care of the kids and keep them in school at that point. I learned to shrimp by myself, and run the boat without any help. This was a little more difficult and dangerous, but I did what I had to do. I wore a ski belt for flotation should I happen to fall overboard. I did this at the request of my wife and my mother. At times I had a deckhand to help out when there were a lot of shrimp, and I couldn't handle the job by myself. Most of the time, however, I could handle the job of running the boat all by myself, and was able to make money and support my family without help. Then, in the middle 80's, government thrust Vietnamese refugees upon us, and the handwriting was on the wall, shrimping was over for us. There was already some overcrowding in the shrimping industry during the middle 80's. At times, there was not enough shrimp for the existing shrimp boat fleet. Then, hundreds of Vietnamese immigrants were set up in the shrimping business up and down the Texas Gulf Coast by our government. To allow them the best chance to be successful, no regulations were enforced against them for several years. As a result, they worked day and night, hauling tons of shrimp out of the bays. They devastated the shrimp population, leaving little for the native shrimp boat fleet to catch. The laws were still enforced rigidly for us. The Vietnamese raped and plundered, while we starved. <u>Your</u> government did this to us. If you want to know more about this, you can read my book, *Dangerous Waters*. I will say no more about that in this book. I sold my boat, and this episode in my life was over. Sometimes hard work just isn't enough, but there are options as you will see.

One day we were visiting my wife's sister and her husband at their home during our off season. We visited them quite often, and they came to our place frequently too. They got us started playing video games. We enjoyed playing the Mario Brothers series, and had a lot of fun together. Later, I would learn to play the Halo series of games, and have really enjoyed these games too. Anyway, my son was playing with their son who was about the same age, and doing something they should not have been doing, running in the house. There was some lumber in the hallway, as my brother-in-law was doing some remodeling in the house. My nephew and son came running down the hallway barefoot on top of this pile of lumber, and my son picked up a splinter from one of the boards. It wasn't just an ordinary splinter though. The wood splinter went in my son's foot just behind the toes, and went just under the skin all the way to the middle of his foot. There was about a quarter inch of wood sticking out, and as my wife held our son, I grabbed the end of the splinter with a pair of pliers and pulled the splinter out. This splinter was just shy of four inches long and has to be a world record. Pulling this splinter out was one of the most painful things I have done, as I knew I was hurting my son, but it had to be done. Luckily the injury did not get infected, and there were no long term effects from the splinter.

What do you say we try another test? This is the easiest algebra test I can think of, to test your math skills. If you have any math skill at all, you should be able to get all four problems correct. They involve addition, subtraction, multiplication, and division. Good luck!

a. $(x + y)$
   $+ (x + y)$
   $\overline{\quad ? \quad}$

b. $(x + y)$
   $- (x + y)$
   $\overline{\quad ? \quad}$

c. $(x + y)$
   $\times (x + y)$
   $\overline{\quad ? \quad}$

d. $(x + y)$
   $/ (x + y)$
   $\overline{\quad ? \quad}$

Answers on page 150

Me with two flathead catfish

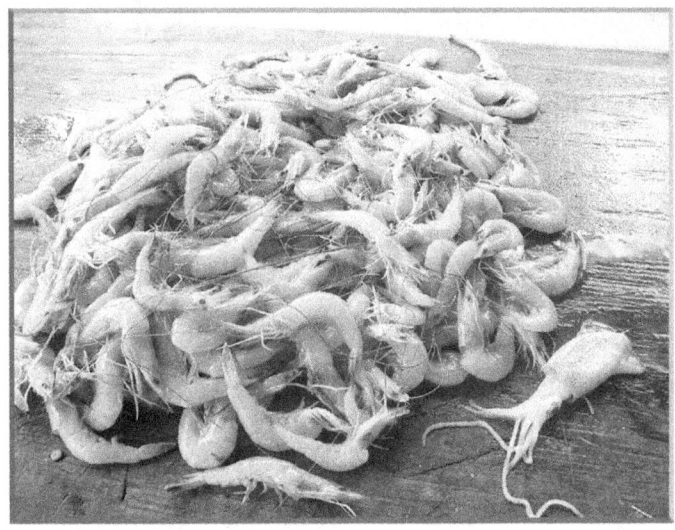
White shrimp and one squid

Sack of net coming aboard with our catch

Checking the net

Shrimping 143

Dumping a load of shrimp?

A nice haul of shrimp this time!

Babysitting was part of the job

Daughter spots a boat!

Shrimping 145

Willie, my best buddy for many years

Me with a pet (Dandy) when I was younger

Chapter 18
Salesman

A new chapter in my life began in the fall of 1989. I sold my boat, and the only job I had was a little fishing. I had been basically unemployed for months, and had no idea what I was going to do with my life. I only knew I had to do something, as just fishing in the river was not sufficient. This was basically part time work. I had a family to support and really had no idea about what to do, but I did know I had to find a job or new career. One day I found a little ad in one of the local newspapers, run by the manufacturer of some type of petroleum products, and they needed a local salesman. I had never been a salesman, and did not even know if I wanted to be a salesman. I answered the ad and they sent me a satchel of information about their company, their products and what they were looking for. As I had nothing else on the plate, I decided to give it a try. I studied the materials they sent, which included all the information I needed to become a salesman of many different types of high grade commercial coatings. This included coatings for roofs, asphalt pavement, masonry coatings, products for coating metal, and some specialty products. By January 1990, I felt I had learned enough to get started, mainly by doing a lot of reading. So I got out and went door to door with my information, brochures and samples and tried to peddle the products.

What I found out very quickly, was selling these products was not going to be easy. I did make a few sales, but they were not large and I was not making much money. Most of the time I was told NO, over and over again NO! The manufacturer had a little program for newcomers, which included an invitation to the President of the Company's ranch in east Texas if I could sell enough products by April, thus showing a little promise I could succeed as a salesman. I did barely manage to meet their quota, and I was offered an invitation to Springtree, the name of this farm. This was a working cattle ranch with cattle, horses, pastures and woods. There were numerous rooms where people could stay, in a couple bunkhouses and in the main house. I found there were usually about 25 or 30 old and new salesmen from around the world (this company was an international company), attending this function every year, if they qualified through their sales volume to do so. The catered food was unbelievable with monster steaks, fried chicken, barbecue, monster burgers, and fried catfish with all the trimmings. The desserts were out of this world—pudding, cobbler and pies loaded with meringue. Some of the food was even cooked on site. But there was a lot more than just food. There were two business sessions and demonstrations where I learned a lot, but best of all were the new friendships, with people from all over the world, who were doing the same thing I was trying to do, and being successful at it.

There were some friendly competitive games and we played pool, threw horseshoes, shot skeet, played ping pong, and of course played poker at night. This was a setting where we could learn in a friendly and fun atmosphere, and that was the purpose of the get together. There were some tall stories told and plenty of beer consumed. I no longer drank beer and this was never a problem. There was also a soft drink cooler that never ran dry, just as the beer cooler never ran dry.

The best thing to come out of this first time at Springtree was a fellow I met, who had been selling the products for four years, but this was also his first year at Springtree. He lived in east Texas, not all that far from the ranch, but never attended, though he could have. When we were not eating or in a business session, we were talking about the business that Johnny had been doing for four years, and I had just begun. We talked for hours on end to after midnight every night, and we became very good friends. The biggest thing I learned was I needed to get into the application of the products I was trying to sell. The commissions were good on the products, but there was an equal amount to be earned in applying them, thus doubling my income. Johnny told me I was strong, and able to do the work, so why should I be giving this money to someone else to apply the products. He was exactly right. I was giving away half the money I could potentially earn. The company of course wanted salesmen, not applicators, and was geared to teach people how to be salesmen. They wanted us to sell and hire outside applicators, but what I learned at Springtree, was most of the men who were successful with the company, were involved in product application.

When I got back home, a few pounds heavier from all the good food and desserts, with a new and very good friend with whom I would talk on the phone at least a couple times a week, and a little more knowledge about the products and how to sell them, I jumped into application with both feet, and started a new company to not only sell the products, but to apply them. It was tough at first, and the sales were not all that good, but I did manage to make a reasonable showing and make a little money along the way. I did not sell a lot of jobs, mostly roof jobs, and applied most of the products myself, as I was not generating enough business to hire someone to help me. Selling and then applying the products made me a better salesman, and I eventually sold more and bigger jobs, not just for roof work, but also for masonry products, paving products, and some of the specialty products. I could then hire local people to help me.

What I was selling, which set me apart from the competition, was maintenance rather than replacement. Periodic maintenance in the form of repairs and coatings would make roofs, paving, masonry and floors last longer and perform better. This in turn would save the customers money over the long term, and this is what I mostly sold. Patch and repair, which is also maintenance, extends the life of roofs, floors, masonry or paving by keeping water out and the problems water can cause. I did a lot of repairs, but the real money was in total coating protection and I began doing a lot more of that too. I had a few replacement options, but that is what everyone else was selling. And though I sold a few replacements, my niche was in coatings. The coatings were good for me, and they were good for the customer.

During my second year selling the products and application of the products, I did not qualify to go to Springtree, as the qualifying quota for second and subsequent year salesmen was higher than for first year salesmen. I vowed to never miss Springtree again after missing the quota that second year. It took about three years to get good at the application of the products, and to sell even more and bigger jobs. I developed a reputation I was honest, hardworking, dependable and I would stand behind the work. If there was a problem, it was usually a labor problem, not a problem with the products, as they were very good high performance products, and generally did not fail due to lack of quality. They were durable and if there was a failure, it was a failure in my performance, but after time I made sure there was no failure in my performance of the work, or in the performance of the men working for me. We did the job right with good products and the customers were happy, and gave us more business down the road.

Early in my new career, I did five little jobs for a bank on the roofs of some of their ATM's. The work was done very well by me alone, as there was not much room on the small ATM roofs. Partly due to my work on these small roofs, I was able to land a very large job with the bank, which gave my business a big boost. I was able to sell this job because of my honesty and integrity, but one of the main things which sold the job, I was told by the Senior Vice-President of the bank, was I did not say anything bad about the competitor I was bidding against, and secondly because of the work I had done on several of their small ATM's, with which they were very pleased. All I did was tout my products and my abilities. My competitor for this project, on the other hand, bad mouthed my products and tried to wine and dine the maintenance manager to get the job. When I was asked about his products, all I would say is he sold pretty good products too, but ours were better and I would give them a great job. My cost was 10% higher, but they gave the job to me anyway. The cost of this job was over $50,000, and when finished with this project they gave me another job of the same size, as well as other work afterwards. The best part was I was no longer forced to bid the jobs against anyone else. They just gave me the jobs outright at my price. This was a very big boost to my career. I would go on to sell over a million dollars in products over the years, and continue to add to these sales now. So far I have not missed another Springtree since the second one I missed.

One thing happened which I feel was very unusual with the first big bank job. As it was the main roof on the bank and six stories high with a ten-foot masonry and metal wall all the way around, materials had to be taken up to the roof and trash down off the roof only on weekends via the elevators when the bank was closed. I did not have a problem with this, but the strange thing was they gave me a set of keys to the bank. We could not get into all areas of the bank, but most of it. Of course, I would never have done anything to lose the trust they had in me, but they could never have been 100% certain of this. I never saw a single guard all the time we worked at the bank on weekends, not inside the bank, or outside. I just think this was very strange and unusual.

Answers to problems on page 140

a. $2x+2y$
b. 0
c. $x^2+2xy+y^2$
d. 1

Chapter 19
New House

About this same time, when I was trying to build a new career, I began building a house with some inheritance money my dad left me when he died the day after Christmas in 1988. I built the home adjacent to my trailer house here on the river, and built it high enough I never expected to get water inside, even though it did once a few years after we moved in. Luckily, there was no carpet on the floors yet, and there was only minimal damage. This was one of four hundred-year floods I would experience. One occurred in 1967 and three in a matter of a few years very close together during this time, but only one got into my home. The others came very close. While there is always the possibility water will once again get high enough to get into my home, the probability is very small, especially in light of the fact that hundred-year floods are supposed to occur only once every hundred years, and I have already experienced four.

I built the home strong enough to survive the winds of small to moderate tornadoes and hurricanes, and so far, I seem to have done well in this respect. We had one hurricane which hit us dead center with one hundred mile per hour winds. The eye passed over the house. There was only minimal damage to the porch. One ash tree could not take the wind and ended up on top of my porch, which crinkled one sheet of the metal roof. I used treated lumber in the walls on the lower levels, so in case they got wet, they would not rot. This is also good protection from termites; while they are not swarming all over the area, I have seen some around. Hopefully, I will not have too many termite problems. So far, so good!

We had outgrown the mobile home we lived in, though it was newer and larger than our original one. It was getting pretty old and had a lot of problems, and it was time for it to go. Our trailer was very near the highway, and the traffic was noisy, especially at night when it was more noticeable. I decided to build my new home about a hundred yards behind this trailer, and a little farther from the noisy highway. I did not have many of the skills needed to build a home, but that didn't stop me. I was determined. I had been planning on building a home for many years, and had worked up plans which changed many times over the years. These plans were constantly changing, as I wanted to build the perfect home for us. Now that I could build the home and had to build the home, as the mobile home we were living in was no longer big enough, and was literally falling down around us, I began the project. I bought a book about building additions, as it contained good and sufficient information about building a home from the foundation up, and with all the different types of rooms in a house. I studied for a while, then began by getting a new electricity pole installed, and began on the foundation.

Living in a mobile home for many, many years taught me one thing, and this was that I wanted to live on a solid foundation, not one up off the ground. Every time you get out of bed the house shakes; every time you walk down the hallway the house shakes; every time you do you know what, the house shakes. I was just tired of the house always shaking, though I blocked the trailer good and was always shimming it up here and there. Also, the floors were made of particle board. The leaky roof and windows, which literally dissolved the floor in places, were a constant problem. If you do not know what particle board is, then I'll tell you. It is the sorriest excuse for man-made plywood that has ever existed on this planet. It is pressed sawdust with some type of glue which I think actually absorbs moisture. This will quickly destroy the stuff. If the commode leaked, it also ate up the floor which dissolved with a little water. The same was true under the sink, the dishwasher and the washing machine. Trailers serve the purpose of cheap housing when you are trying to get on your feet, but there is nothing like a well built and durable home with quality material and this is exactly what I was going to build.

The spot I had picked for the home was not big enough for the house I designed, so I hired a dump truck, a dozer and a frontend loader to haul in about 900 cubic yards (3 feet x 3 feet x 3 feet, or 27 cubic feet) of dirt from across the road. The truck packed the ground very hard driving over and over the area, and I continued to haul in dirt until I had widened and raised the level of dirt on the plot to the width, length and height I figured would be high enough to keep the water out of the house. I got out my plans and my book, and learned how to frame out the foundation and level it up, dig the trenches, install the plumbing and drain lines, install the electricity and gas lines, and covered it with plastic film for a moisture barrier, and install rebar. I did this all by myself, which was very hard work and time consuming as well, but I did it and I did it right.

Then I was ready to pour concrete. I hired a few hands to help with this task. The concrete was poured in three stages, and the help I hired were not much help, but I could not have done it without them. Everyone claimed to know how to pour concrete, but when the time came to pour, they didn't know squat and are ready for a break after ten minutes' work. That is not the way it works with concrete. You take a break when the concrete tells you that you can take a break, which is maybe in an hour when the concrete is smooth. The concrete was fairly smooth but not perfect, but it had to do. With carpet you would not notice the minor imperfections. Most of the home would have carpet, but not until years later. Temporarily I painted the bare concrete with grey paint, so it would look a little better and be easier to sweep and keep clean.

I framed out the house and rafters all by myself, and my little book on how to build additions. I was learning by reading and doing, and I did a lot every day. I worked from daylight until after dark sometimes, and after a hard day of work, I had to literally peel my fingers from around my hammer to lay it down. I was using hundreds of pounds of nails, and lost track of how many at about 700 pounds. That is a lot of nails for one hand to drive. Now you know why I had to peel my hand from the hammer every day. I built the roof, I built the walls, I insulated the walls, installed the siding, paneling and sheetrock, all from instructions from my little book. I learned how to install wiring and water and gas lines, installed the appliances, and installed the air conditioning and heating system and all the duct work. I did all of this mostly without any help outside of my little book. I did get a little help with the shingles from a brother-in-law, and a little help from my father-in-law, but I did not hire anyone to help me. I built the home from the ground up all by myself and my little book. This was quite a chore, as the home has five bedrooms, three bathrooms, an office, a laundry room and a garage. The living room area has a cathedral ceiling with an overhead walkway between the upstairs office and bedroom, and also a circular staircase and a fireman's pole to get down if you choose. There are two dormers upstairs, so I could have one window in each of the upstairs rooms. There is also a library over the kitchen area. The dimension of my home is thirty-two feet by eighty-five feet, to give you an idea of how large this place is, and how large an undertaking it was. The roof has a 9/12 pitch, which is nearly a 35-degree slope and just barely walkable. The roof area is 4,300 square feet, or 43 squares, and has ¾-inch plywood decking, at my father-in-law's recommendation. A square is ten feet by ten feet, or 100 square feet if you haven't already figured that out.

 I took off a couple months from work to get the home dried in, and then worked through the wintertime to finish out a couple bedrooms, a bathroom and the kitchen. Then we moved out of the trailer, and into the unfinished home. I worked on the home evenings, after I had finished my other work, and most weekends, and did this for years. I also built a large porch at the rear of the home overlooking the river. I studied my little book, worked on company business in town, and worked on the home when I had time. I paid for the materials as I went along, and when I finished the home, there was no mortgage.

 I had a flatbed trailer I used to haul fish. Now I used it to buy and haul loads of lumber, insulation, and appliances. I did all this work too. I didn't have to load the materials, but did unload all the stuff. Keep in mind I was also working very hard at keeping my business going during this time, and I was doing most of the work at this too, as well as making the sales calls to generate the business I needed. I took it upon myself to work harder than anyone should ever have to work, but this was my choice. I chose to learn how to do the things I needed to know, to do everything necessary to build a home from start to finish, and I did it very well.

    I did have a setback or two. At times there was not enough money to complete a project, and it had to be put on hold for a while, or I managed to contract a large job that needed my full attention, but probably the worst setback was when I hurt my back. I was building trusses, which spanned the entire width of the home, and would stand about twenty-two feet above the floor when slid over the beams running across the rooms, and these trusses were very heavy. I was picking up the last truss to slide it onto the central beam, and when I had the truss up and was sliding it onto the central beam, my back popped and gave way. I managed to get the truss onto the beam but hurt my back very badly. I managed to make it back to the trailer house with a makeshift crutch, and lay down on the couch. The popped vertebrae in my back pinched the sciatic nerve in my lower back, and up to now this was the worst pain I had ever felt. It felt as if someone had stuck a knife in my back, and every time I moved, coughed, sneezed, or anything, someone was twisting the knife. The pain I would not wish on my worst enemy. Well, maybe I would wish it on my <u>worst</u> enemy. The pain lasted for nearly a week, and I did not go to the doctor. The damage also made it impossible for me to sit normally again for any length of time, and from this time on, I stopped taking baths and began taking showers, as I could not sit in the tub comfortably. Showers I now think are better anyway. Though I could now take baths if I wanted, I still only take showers.

    I did get better and resumed the work on my home and business. The next few years were good. I was making money, supporting my family, taking vacations, fishing and basically enjoying life again. I lived in a home I could be proud of, though it wasn't finished. I was gardening and enjoying this, and keeping my yard mowed and enjoying time with my kids. When my son was about eighteen, my son, my nephew and I learned to play golf in the front yard. It was my idea to learn to play golf. We picked some clubs up at a local pawn shop, played in the front yard and taught each other how to play with the help of a rule book and practice. When we thought we were good enough, we went to play at a local golf course. We got pretty good. I was never easy on my son and nephew, and beat them most of the time. I never <u>let</u> them beat me. This proved a good strategy, as my son eventually improved enough to beat me and now I cannot beat him. He can hit the ball farther and straighter than I can, and is much steadier with better eyes and able to make more putts than me. I am happy to say I have made more birdies than he, and even made one eagle, which is two under par for a hole, but my son has made at least two or three eagles. Golf helped keep the kids out of trouble, gave them the opportunity to learn a little patience, and how to concentrate. My son worked at two golf clubs while attending college, and we got to play a free round from time to time at some very swanky courses. The kids finally grew up, and we seldom get the chance to play golf anymore, but it was a good learning experience and we had a lot of fun together. Never say you cannot do anything. Always be positive and if you want to do something, then don't let anything hold you back. Do what you can, and if you don't know how to do something, then learn. Learn by doing, and if it takes some reading, then find the appropriate book and read. Just do it!

 When my older sister died in 1995, and my younger sister and I split up the land our dad left us when he died, I got most of the area adjoining my home, including the area across the road where I wanted to run a few cattle. The remainder of the land I got was leased out, as I did not want to get back into a big cattle operation. Life was good, and life was fun, and I just didn't have the time to get back into the cattle business big time. I was working hard with my business and this was going good, and it would be another year or so before my home would be mostly finished, though it is never completely finished. There is always something that needs to be done. I still needed to put in a lot of time on the home, but I did manage to get a small cattle operation going across the road from the house with a few cattle/pets, and everything seemed to be going good. There wasn't much I wanted to change at this point. Life was just floating along, and I was happy.

We took a trip to Riverside Campground, near Garner State Park west of San Antonio, one summer to have a little fun in the clear water and the cool rapids. My son, nephew and I would float down the river on our inner tubes with our little rods and reels, catching perch and bass all the way down. Sometimes we would get into the little rapids and spin around in our tubes, but we were still fishing and catching fish. My two daughters were also on the trip and liked the tubing, but were not into the fishing. We cooked over an open fire and had a great time. There had been some lightning and rain each night, but every morning everything had cleared up and was nice and sunny again. The rain was elsewhere and did not affect us in the least. We were not concerned about it. But one night the rain was very heavy off in the distance, and though it never rained on us, was just in the right place so all the rainwater came down our valley. We were sleeping on the ground in tents, and one of my daughters woke us up saying there was water in the tent. We all got up immediately and could see the water was rising very, very quickly. We piled into my truck in less than a minute leaving everything behind and dressed as we were. By the time I started the truck, the water had already risen nearly a foot. That night we knew it was going to be bad, as the water was rising an inch in a matter of seconds. The shortest distance to higher ground was straight ahead, so I took off straight ahead for the road I knew was over there. There was a low area between us and the road though. By the time we had gotten into the truck, which could not have been more than a minute or two, the water was already up to the bottom of the truck. We took off through the low area, and when we got to the middle of the dip, the water was deep enough that it came all the way up to the windshield of my truck, and I could feel the tires lose traction as we plowed through the water, which was somewhere around three and a half feet deep. A little I it seemed to me, as I had done this before back in 1967 with my first car. Luckily, the truck engine was diesel with no spark plugs or ignition system to foul out, and the truck engine never sputtered, but I was not sure we could get enough traction with our tires to push us out of the deep and fairly swift water. But we did, just barely I'm sure, make it through, and we breathed a sigh of relief when we made it to dry ground. We were lucky, but there were many who were not.

As we were sitting in the truck watching the water, and it was starting to get daylight, I looked down at the road by the truck and here came the water rushing up the road again. We moved a little farther up the road and up the hill. A guy with a big truck and a big travel trailer was having trouble getting his trailer out. He was afraid the water was going to get up high enough to get to his trailer. He asked if I would give him a pull. I told him to hook a chain onto my truck and I would give it a try. Of course my truck was going to pull him out, it was a Ford. His wife said her husband was a little embarrassed to ask us to give him a pull, as he had a brand new Dodge of which he was very proud, but was not able to do the job. She insisted he ask us for help. His pride could have cost him his truck and trailer. Remember this for future reference. We got his truck and trailer out, and we moved up the hill away from the rising water again. The water kept coming and coming, and as it got daylight we could see trailers floating down the river. Not just a few trailers, but a lot of them. By the time the water had stopped rising, most of the trailers in the valley, and there were a lot of them as this area was a very popular camping area, were lost to the flood.

We left my wife's car behind and all our equipment. We were literally seconds away from possibly losing our lives. We listened to the radio telling of people being rescued out of the trees, as we heard sounds of the rescue helicopters in the air that came to pluck people out of the treetops. These people were lucky too. There were plenty of very tall cypress trees that are generally easy to climb because they have a lot of limbs close together. I don't think anyone died in our campground, but this turned out to be a serious flood, and I think a couple died in some other campgrounds. I think in all, the water rose over thirty feet in a matter of a few hours. My family was very, very lucky. When the water went down, we went back to our campsite and found my wife's car standing on end in a tree. We found very little else of our belongings.

My mother-in-law was having some serious health problems, and my father-in-law was having some health problems of his own, so they came to live with us for a while, as my mother-in-law was too much for my father-in-law to handle alone. We had a couple spare bedrooms. The older kids were in college and had moved out, so we let them move into one of the bedrooms. My father-in-law liked to help around the house and liked to cook as I did, and I had no problem with them moving in. As the house was not completely finished, he offered to help with some of the inside trim work, and I had no problem with this either. They moved in, and we were a big happy family again.

My mother-in-law was a little nutty at times, due to a head injury, and had to be locked in the house much of the time, but my father-in-law always kept a close eye on her, and took very good care of her. One minute she seemed quite normal, and then the next minute she would totally lose it. She got out of the house once. I just happened to be coming home from a job, and as I got close to our road, I saw someone running up the driveway and onto the highway in her nightgown. Guess who that was? I stopped my truck on the side of the road, and ran out onto the highway, grabbed my mother-in-law, and threw her over my shoulder like a sack of potatoes. She was not very big and it was just lucky there was almost no traffic up and down the highway at this time. Well, I took off toward the house with my mother-in-law over my shoulder, her screaming and fighting me the whole way. As I neared the house, I met my wife and father-in-law headed my way. They were shocked she had gotten out, and upon the highway. This was the last time that would happen, as latches were installed at the top of all the outside doors, so my mother-in-law could not reach them. She died not long after, and we found out my father-in-law had terminal cancer, so he didn't live much longer either.

Death is a part of life, and you may as well get used to this. My first experience with death was with my grandmother on my dad's side. I could not face her death, and I don't think anyone understood why I did not attend her funeral, but I had my reasons. I think her death hurt me more than any others. Afterward, I got a grip on death, and understood it was a normal and necessary side of life. I have attended many funerals since my grandmother's, and none of those were hard to deal with. I have even made a few plans for my funeral, and hope it turns out to be the celebration I wish it to be, with music and laughter, not sadness, as I have already lived a full life that should be celebrated, not mourned. I plan and certainly hope to squeeze quite a few more years out of life, but when I go it will be my time, and I just hope I go quickly. A slow death from cancer or something like that is not a way I would want to leave this world.

My mother is currently still living, and is quite old. My stepdad died, and my mother is largely blind from macular degeneration, and living alone. Almost everyone she has known, including one daughter, is dead. She is miserable. Only death will probably ease her misery. If she could see better, it might be a little different. It is really surprising though, she can still function around the house. Her mentality is the main problem, but she cannot help the way she has become. It could be worse though. My sister and I cannot do much to ease her pain. Remember, if you live almost forever, as my mother has, health problems, and mental problems especially, will become a major challenge. My mom's senility almost gets the best of me from time to time, but I bite my tongue and keep my mouth shut. You need to be nice to old people. Their age dictates their actions. I know I certainly don't want to live as long as she has, with problems like hers. Too long a life causes too many problems, and too much misery.

Chapter 20
Tank Accident

Life seems to be a roller coaster ride, and when things are going great and you reach a pinnacle point, the roller coaster suddenly takes a nose dive. That just seems to be the way life is, and though the ups and downs are seldom extremes, there will be extreme dips in life, and it is something all of us must learn to accept. It is not pleasant, but it is something I have come to accept, and have learned to cope with. Sometimes it might be the tiny ups and downs, which are never ending, that get to you. Sometimes it may be the big dips that get to you, but whichever, you must learn to accept first, and then cope with these disasters, large and small. If you cannot cope, life will be miserable. You have the strength to cope, but you may need to dig very deeply into your bag of gifts to find this strength.

Things were going along great when disaster struck again on December 8, 2000. I was working on a job in a nearby city installing a roof system. This particular roof was a single-ply membrane, torch down roof system. The single-ply is heated with a roofing torch on the bottom side of the membrane, to melt it together and to the roof surface. The roof system was mostly finished. The roof surface was finished, and it only lacked the flashing areas around the perimeter of the roof, before putting on the final protective and reflective coating. The perimeter work was to seal the roof surface membrane to the metal edge trim, with heated strips of the roofing membrane. A propane torch was used to heat the strips cut from the roll of membrane. The tools and freshly filled propane bottle were taken to the roof, and placed in the middle of the roof. A couple hours later, I had finished a lot of other little tasks which needed to be done first, and was ready to begin the finish work around the perimeter of the roof. I walked over to the center of the roof, where the propane tank was sitting with the regulator and rubber hose attached, and ready to go. I went to pick up and move the propane tank to the edge of the roof, and when I touched it, the tank exploded. The propane bottle broke into two pieces around the middle of the bottle where there was a weld, and the top half of the bottle hit me around the belt line. It hit my hand as well, and did a little damage to my hand, but the bulk of the damage was to my pelvis, which was shattered, and my waistline was ripped open from hip to hip. Also my bladder was ruptured by the force of the explosion, the inside of both my legs were ripped open, and one of my testicles was ripped out and damaged beyond repair. The explosion knocked me out, and threw me about ten feet from where I was standing. I was only out a few seconds, and woke up on my back to see the white cloud of propane gas rising into the air above me. The gas did not ignite, or else I would have burned up on the roof, and this book would never have been written.

I remember the damaged area of my body felt very cold. This was due to the liquid propane which spilled onto me. I looked down to see my blue jeans shredded from the explosion. There was little blood, and it was a good thing I was not bleeding badly, or I could have bled to death right there on the roof. I was not in a lot of pain, but I knew I was badly hurt. I used my arms to drag my numb and not functioning lower half, to the edge of the roof where the ladder had been set up, as this is where it would be necessary to get me off the building. I then waited for help to arrive, as there was nothing else I could do. I certainly could not get off the roof on my own. My legs didn't seem to work at the moment.

    The EMS station was about a mile down the road, and they said they heard the explosion and were ready, as they knew someone had to be hurt in the explosion, when the call came in. My helper who was on the roof with me, was startled by the explosion but not hurt, and called out to a lady across the street to call the EMS, when she came out of her house after hearing the explosion. She made the call and the

EMS got there quickly, though it seemed like a long time to me, as I was beginning to feel some pain. The EMS technician cut my jeans off and assessed the situation. He asked me a few questions to check my mental condition, and got me off the roof and into the ambulance quickly. I was awake and knew what was going on the entire time. We had a second ladder on my truck, and the crew set this other ladder up beside the one that was already there, put me in a basket, and slid me down the ladders. I was not in a lot of pain so far, as I was still pretty well numbed by the shock of the explosion, and talked to the EMS members as they worked at getting me off the roof and into the ambulance. It took a few minutes, but they got me into the ambulance and off we went to a neighboring city. There was no hospital in the fishing community where the accident happened.

It took about an hour to get me to the hospital and into the operating room, from the time of the explosion, and the pain got worse during the ambulance trip, as I was beginning to feel some of the damage done to my body. Every little bump the ambulance hit would send more pain through my riddled body, and it seemed like a really long time before we finally got to the hospital. I remember seeing the surgeon, and him telling me to count backwards from a hundred. I said one hundred, ninety-nine, and I was out. They put me out quickly, and the next thing I remember was waking up in intensive care. I spent four days in intensive care, and don't really remember a lot about these four days, as I was drugged heavily. It didn't seem like I was there for more than a day, but they said four days.

They finally thought I was stable enough to move to a private room, but this is not the end of the story. I was given some food and really didn't have much of an appetite yet, but I did eat some. The doctor finally realized my intestines had stopped working. I do not want to get too gross in what happened after this, but they did get them working again, with a lot of enemas. The worst part was, when they found out my intestines were not working, they had no choice but to take me off all food. The food I had already eaten had fermented inside me, and I became very bloated. They ran a tube down my throat and into my stomach, and it gushed some of the nastiest stuff I have ever seen or smelled, but it did relieve the pressure and bloating. They kept the tube in for a few days, and for four days I only had a cup of ice to eat. I wanted more, but I didn't get it. I got really hungry, but could not eat until my intestines started working again. When they finally got my intestines working, and I was allowed to eat something, I was put on a liquid diet. This included tea, gelatin, gravy, and popsicles. The first thing I ate was the brown beef roast gravy. This tasted a little salty, and after not having anything to eat for four days, it was the best thing I have ever tasted. I know it probably wasn't that good, but to me it was like a perfectly seasoned and cooked ribeye steak.

Some of the drugs I was getting were pretty crazy too, in that one in particular made me hallucinate badly. I can still remember one dream which was really nuts. I remember I had to roll string into a ball, and as I rolled the string into a ball, the ball kept getting bigger and bigger, and the string itself kept getting bigger and became too large for me to handle, but I couldn't stop though I do not know why. I couldn't stop, but I also could not continue, and this was very frustrating and driving me nuts.

I was also in a good deal of pain, even with the morphine I was taking regularly. I was given a control button, to control the amount of morphine I could take, and it seemed like I was pushing this button every fifteen or twenty minutes. I was taking all the machine would give me. I think I had about a gallon of morphine during my hospital stay. It almost took away the pain at times, but not quite, and I could really tell when the morphine began to wear off just a little bit. Since my pelvis was broken in half, and the surgeon decided to let it grow back together on its own, the pain was almost unbearable when I was moved to change the bed linens, or had to go out for a cat scan. Every time they would try to move me, the pieces of my pelvis would grate together, and the pain was almost enough to knock me out. They finally brought me a bed with a trapeze, which helped a lot, as I still had a lot of strength in my upper body. With the trapeze, I could pull myself straight up without twisting, so the nurses could change the bed linens, and also to help myself get out of bed. I was in control with the trapeze. I could do things on my own, and the pain was a lot less.

To help get my intestines working again, in addition to the many enemas, they began some light physical therapy, which mostly consisted of walking and also sitting up in a chair, rather than just lying in bed all the time. I couldn't get out of my bed without help, and I couldn't even stand up without help. But this little oriental gal strapped a belt around me, and they gave me a walker, and off we went. We walked to the door and back at first, and after this short walk I was exhausted. My legs were very weak and I could just barely stand with the help of the walker, but the little oriental gal assured me she could catch me if I was to fall, but I seriously had my doubts. She couldn't have weighed more than 90 pounds, and I was over 200. We never had to test whether or not she could hold me up, and I tried my best not to fall. She got me going enough after a few days, to take a walk down the hallway and back. The trip was not very long, maybe 50 feet, and I was really happy to get back into bed. I never got a foot off the floor, as my feet and legs were so weak, I didn't have the strength to lift the weight of my legs. I could hold myself up with the walker, and scooted my feet enough to move forward, but this was the extent of my walking ability.

The time came when I needed a shower, but could not do this task on my own as I still had to hold onto the walker with both hands to keep from falling. My legs were not a lot of help, and I relied mostly on my arms to hold myself up with the walker. The little oriental therapist took on this task, and she helped me into the shower and removed my hospital gown. The warm water running over my body felt so good, as I was scrubbed from head to toe. I just stood there and enjoyed, and she didn't appear to be the least bit embarrassed by the task. I felt a little life in the once dead organs, when she cleaned my private parts. This really felt good, and I did not let on I was having any feelings in this previously dead area, and she never knew because there was still too much damage from the accident to get an erection. I wasn't about to tell her either.

My doctor told me the accident looked like something he would expect to see in wartime. All the tissue around my injury had solidified and was hard as concrete, like a giant blood/fat clot. My doctor said he had expected I would die, as my injuries were extensive. What he didn't know was how tough I was, from a lifetime of hard work. I never expected to die, and never felt mentally like I would die, but probably came pretty close to doing so. Finally, I was told there was nothing else they could do for me, and I was released. I thanked the doctor for everything he had done in saving my life, and even went and looked up the little oriental therapist, and gave her a big hug too. There was a little Florence Nightingale effect going on here I think.

Everything was working again on the inside, and I could just barely walk or scoot with the walker, when I was taken home. But the ordeal was not even close to being over. In fact, the ordeal was just beginning. I went through weeks of therapy to learn to walk again, and spent most of my time in a recliner or in bed. I ate good, pooped good and worked very hard to learn to walk again. The therapy was tough and painful, and it didn't seem like I was making much progress over the weeks ahead, but slowly and steadily I was walking again. It was very frustrating to lie in bed, and try to do a leg lift for the therapist, and not be able to get my leg off the bed. I did try though it was painful, and I continued to try, not just with the therapist, but also when he was not there. Very slowly I got better, and eventually I got rid of the walker. It got to the point I could walk with a cane.

I did everything I could to get back into shape again. But I didn't want to just be able to walk again. I wanted to be able to do things again, to be able to work again, at least to some extent. I worked hard to get back into a reasonable shape. I would walk and walk to get strength back into my legs. I would practice getting in and out of my truck, so I would be able to drive again. I would later go up and down my spiral staircase, and even later I would climb up and down the ladder at jobsites, where my son-in-law was now doing the jobs I could no longer do. I would do things around the house that needed to be done, but doing them as much to get back into shape, as for the fact they were things which needed attention. Being in good physical shape through a lifetime of hard work helped me survive this accident, and now I was again working as hard as I was able, to get back into at least a good portion of my original shape. I never got back all my strength, but have recovered at least 50-60% of my original strength, and this is enough to function, do chores around the house and a little outside work, but not nearly enough I could ever run my business again. I am still technically disabled, though you would not know it by looking at me. But can I work a job again? Maybe, if I were allowed to take enough breaks. I can do a lot of things, but there are many things I can no longer do, and I have little stamina. My pelvis and back are a constant source of pain, but no more than a little arthritis. This is something I have come to accept and live with.

My accident has given me a greater respect for others who have lost a limb or two, but continue to strive to better themselves. Never let a little handicap get in your way. Even if you have a huge handicap, live your life the best you can. Then there are those, who while seemingly perfectly healthy, have their little self-inflicted mental or physical handicaps, who really screw up their lives. This includes you fat pigs out there, who can't do anything simply because you are fat. Don't make excuses for not living life to its fullest. If you are one of these people, and you do not care enough to exert the energy necessary to improve yourself, you will get no pity from me.

Chapter 21
Poker

My son-in-law took over most of the work in my business after my accident, as I could do nothing. He needed a job, and I needed someone to do my work for me, so I made him a proposition he could not refuse. I taught him all I could and would visit the job sites and show him what needed to be done, and while he did most of the work fairly well, he was not me. I kept the business going because he needed the job, and while I was reaping some benefits from the business, the company was not making any money. I hoped he would eventually make me and the company some money, but after probably a few years too many, I finally saw this was not going to happen. As my son-in-law was not able to do the task at hand, at the level I was able to perform before my accident, I eventually closed the business. I did not need the business. My insurance settlement allowed me to retire.

Somewhere along the way, probably around 2004, I started playing poker online. I played on one of the popular sites, and played real money tournaments mostly, but also played a little in the cash games. In tournaments, you buy in for whatever the tournament fee for the particular tournament happens to be. You then play until there is one winner. There can be only one winner, but usually the top ten percent get paid, but lesser amounts than the winner. In cash games, you buy in and play until you lose your money, or get tired of playing. I really liked the Texas No-Limit Hold'em games, and these are what I played most of the time. I got pretty good at it. I could hold my own with most players, and when I got beat, it was usually because someone sucked out on me, as I usually had the best hand early on. This game can be frustrating at times, but it is also a very fast and fun game too. I didn't lose much money along the way, so I could afford the game really easily. It got to the point I wanted to play some live games, so I ventured off to a casino in Louisiana. It was a pretty good distance to this casino, but casino gambling was not, and is not, allowed in my state, Texas. There are too many holier than thou assholes in Texas to allow a casino to be built. I say they have no right to tell me, or anyone else for that matter, what I can and cannot do with my own money. They say otherwise. But Louisiana and others say I can. It is not right to not be able to play Texas No Limit Hold'em in Texas!

I played in tournaments and some cash games, mostly limit games, but after a while I learned in limit games, you had to play against too many players in each hand, which led to too many suck-outs at the end of the hand. I began to play mostly no limit hold'em from then on. Limit and no limit hold'em are the same game, with the only difference being in the amount of betting. The only limit in no limit is the amount of money you have on the table in front of you. In limit hold'em, you are limited to a specific bet before and after the flop, and then a different and usually higher bet after the turn and river cards. You can make a raise when someone bets, but the amount of the raise can only be the amount of the specific limit bet at the time the bet is placed. This may be a little confusing, but if you were to play a little, you would be able to understand the betting easily and very quickly.

No limit and limit hold'em are poker games where you get two initial cards, and then play five community cards, as does everyone else, placed on the poker table by the dealer. The first three community cards are called the flop, then the dealer places a fourth card called the turn, and a final fifth card called the river card, with a round of betting before the flop, after the flop, after the turn card, and a final round of betting after the river card. If you have a really good hand with your two initial cards and the three flop cards, you are generally better off if you can push other players out of the hand, before they make a better hand to beat you with the turn and river cards. You are also better off playing against one opponent, rather than three or four. This is more difficult to control in limit poker, and more easily accomplished in a no limit game, when you can bet much more and force your opponents to fold before the flop, or before they suck out on you with a better hand after the flop. There is a lot of strategy in betting, and while there is some luck to all poker games, this is a skills game where you need a good poker face and bluffing abilities, but you also need to catch a few good hands and a few good breaks from time to time. This is the luck part, which is also part of the game.

One day my poker buddy, who often played at this casino in Louisiana, and we even planned trips there together, said "hey, let's go to Vegas." It sounded like a good idea to me, though I had never been on a jet and really didn't care to fly. I was unsure about flying, but didn't hesitate long, and I said OK. I booked a trip to Las Vegas and in August 2007 I was set to go. I tried to get my wife to go, but she refused. We had not gotten along for years, though we tolerated each other and continued to live together. I didn't have anything to keep me from Las Vegas. I wanted to live again, which I had not done for a long time. Mostly I worked, played online poker, and did a few things with the kids when this was possible, but I did nothing with my wife—nothing! This wasn't my choice, but hers. We didn't talk much and we didn't do things together, we just lived separate lives together. We used to fight a lot when we were younger, mostly about money, but didn't even do this much anymore. We just got unhappily along.

While I was in Las Vegas, I stayed at Harrah's Casino and Hotel. I played in thirteen small cash tournaments in five days. I didn't play elsewhere, because I was doing well where I was at. I finished in first twice, second place once, third place twice, and fourth and fifth places, cashing in on seven out of thirteen tournaments, and made a pocket full of money. I thought to myself this was pretty good, and because of this first trip and the success I had, I returned every month for the next year. I tried to get my wife to go, but she wouldn't have anything to do with me, or Las Vegas.

The trips to Las Vegas were much more than just the gambling though. Even though I am not a city guy, and really don't care much for being in the city, Las Vegas was much different. It was not just a city to me, it was an experience. Las Vegas is so alive with people walking around everywhere, doing things and going places in a constant party mode, and there is so much to see. I took my camera most of the time, and besides playing poker, I was also the tourist, taking pictures of just about everything I came across that was interesting, and interesting things were everywhere I turned. My camera was also capable of taking movies, and I took plenty of movies too. Looking back at some of the photos, I really looked like the tourist, always wearing shorts and tennis shoes.

I also dressed the same when I was playing poker, and I think this played to my advantage at times. I think most people underestimated my poker abilities, and I continue to play on this look. I am not afraid to play poker against anyone, and I certainly hope they underestimate my poker abilities. I get terribly unlucky at times, and sometimes a trap will blow up in my face and I'll lose badly, but I am a good player and will do good most of the time when I play, however, the odds are always against you when you are playing in a tournament against thousands. Your odds of winning are never good in a large tournament, but your odds are just as good as everyone else, and everyone has an equal chance of winning. I think my odds are just a little bit better than most. Call me the optimist.

One very important thing I have learned over the years, is only <u>you</u> can make <u>you</u> happy. I was happy when I played live poker and online poker, and I was happy when I was flying. I wanted to have fun, and I did what I needed to do to have all the fun I could, and this was playing poker. If you learn nothing else from reading this book, you should learn that if you are not happy, you should change your life, even drastically if necessary. It is very important to be happy. I still did a fair amount of work, mostly chores around the house, but I played poker every chance I got. Be happy! If you are not, then do what you need to do to get there.

To take a phrase from the Forrest Gump movie, life is like a box of chocolates, you never know what you are going to get.

This may be true in some respects, but you can also guide your life in most areas. I did not know I was going to have a very serious accident in 2000 and very nearly die, but I had a choice when it came to getting better and getting back into a decent shape, so I could function and take care of myself. And I didn't know my wife would decide she no longer wanted to live with me, and she walked out in early 2008. She just packed up and left, as she found another guy online who had moved from Florida to Texas to be with her. That was fine with me. We had not had a life together for years though we did live together. I basically told her to not let the door hit her in the butt, and that was that. Our divorce was final on June 20, 2008, and I was free of her for the most part. I say for the most part, because we still talk and get along, because of the kids and grandkids. We probably get along better now than we have for many years. We had a very easy and equitable divorce, and we are both happy as far as I know. I know for sure, I am happy.

I would not trade our divorce for anything, but I also would not trade our life together for anything either. The reason is we had three very beautiful and smart kids together. My ex spent a lot of time with the kids making certain they grew up smart. I hope I taught them a few things too. I think we spent more time with our kids than the average family today. They were always loved and they knew they were loved. They were also raised to be responsible and never got into trouble. I have been told many times we have the <u>best</u> kids, and they really are good kids. They were well behaved when they were growing up, and I think this reflects on the parents. If your kids are not so good, then maybe it's not the kids, but you. I would not trade our kids for anything. I think we were responsible parents, and the result was three responsible young adults. Do your maintenance, and just maybe your kids won't come back to haunt you later in life. Think about it.

Me hard at work on a local roof

Me at the WSOP

Chapter 22
Iceland

I began playing more poker in Las Vegas, and started playing in a few of the World Series of Poker (WSOP) events, as well as numerous cash tournaments, and did fairly well for the most part, but not so well in the WSOP games. I did do quite well at the "sit and go" (single table tournament) tables, and won several entries into the WSOP events, as well as some cash, but came up a bit short when I got to the big tournaments. There was plenty of time to catch a few hands, as the tournaments play pretty slow when the blinds are small. It just seemed I could not catch enough good hands, and you certainly can't bluff all the time, so basically I just blinded out. The blinds are forced bets, placed on the table before each hand is dealt. These blinds stimulate action and increase as the tournament progresses. When players are dealing cards in home games, everyone gets his turn as dealer. When there is a dealer who is not playing in the game as in casinos, there is a dealer button, usually a white disc, used to represent each player one at a time as the dealer, and moves clockwise from player to player on each hand dealt. The small blind is the first player to the left of the dealer button, and the big blind is the second player to the left of the button. As poker tournaments progress, the blinds get larger and larger. If you do not win enough hands, and continually lose chips as a result of the blinds, you eventually blind out. The blinds remain the same throughout a cash game. I like to play 1-2 or 1-3 no limit. The small blind stays at $1, and $2 or $3 for the big blind. The $2 or $3 big blinds vary from casino to casino. These are small stakes, but I do not need big stakes to have fun. For me, the game is all about fun.

I was having fun in Las Vegas and at home, but there was also something lacking in my life which had been lacking for a very long time, but was more apparent now that my wife was gone, and I was living in my large and very empty home alone. What I was lacking was a woman. Las Vegas was full of women, and nakedness was everywhere I turned, but this is not what I wanted in a woman. They were very nice to look at, but for the most part were young, skinny little things wearing outfits which left very little to the imagination, and this was not what I was looking for. The search was on for the next Mrs. Landgraf, or at least so I thought. I found I had become very particular, and didn't know if that special woman was even out there, but I began my search.

I met a gal on an online poker site, and thought she might be the one. One thing was certain, we had one thing in common, poker, and she was good too. We spent hours and days and weeks talking to each other, and playing poker online together. We got to know each other very well. She was a widow with one daughter, good looking and seemed very sweet. She had some health problems, which included kidney disease, among others. When she suddenly disappeared, and I didn't hear from her for weeks on end, I decided I would go see her. Now that I really enjoyed flying, I got a passport and headed to Iceland. This was my first trip out of the country, and I really enjoyed the trip, but what I found was heartbreaking. She had died, and it took me a while to get over this ordeal, but I didn't let this ruin my first trip out of the country. The trip to Iceland was an eye-opening trip, and I really enjoyed the island country and meeting new and different people, seeing new sights and experiencing a new culture. Of course, I had my camera and have a good photo history of my trip there.

While I have taken a few trips to border towns into Mexico just south and west of where I live, I don't consider these trips as actually going out of the country. A mile or so out of the country, at least, is not very far out of the country. I consider the trip to Iceland my first real trip out of the USA. I took this first and only trip to Iceland, arriving there in early November. It was fairly cold when I got there. The temperature was above freezing, but cold nevertheless. The weather was foggy and drizzly and damp. The first thing I noticed about the country, after my half hour drive from the airport in Keflavik to the capital city of Reykjavik, was the city was very clean. I didn't see any trash on the streets anywhere, and many of the streets were paved with bricks. The rest of the streets were paved with volcanic rock. The tires on the cars were ice tires, and made a scratching sound when they drove over the brick roads. The mostly three to five story buildings were quaint and colorfully painted, and the little city seemed quite cozy and easy to navigate. There were statues and sculptures all over the place, and some of them were quite large, especially the one in front of their central church. I have photos of most of them. The area in front of the church was also paved with small stones, mostly gray with white accent stones. I liked meandering around the harbor and looking at the whaling ships, and the ducks floating around in corners of the harbor. The entire coastline was lined with huge blocks of volcanic rock extending at least fifteen feet above the water's edge.

Walking and bicycle trails were everywhere, and they were all paved and lighted. The November days were relatively short, due to the island country's proximity to the Arctic Circle, and dawn and twilight seemed to run together, with no mid-day in the middle. It just stayed a little gloomy all day long most days, but the sun did come out from time to time. Anyway, I walked these paths every day, taking photos all along the way. There were streams with white water and a flock of geese here and there. The water was green and clear. There was sleet around and along the pathways, but it never snowed while I was there. One night when I was out, a cold north wind blew in, and blew a gale. The wind chill factor had to be well below zero, and I was not dressed for it. It was a miserable walk, the two or three miles in the dark, to my hotel. There were some places near buildings where it was difficult to walk into the wind, which had to be blowing 50 mph or more.

When I got up the next morning and walked over to the

central lake there in Reykjavik, I found it had completely frozen over, with about a half inch or more of ice. The waves in the lake were even frozen, and the lake had little ice waves. There was a bicycle frozen in the water at one end of the lake. The ducks and geese which frequented the lake, and apparently spent a lot of time there playing and feeding in the water, were walking all over the ice. After a while, there was one corner of the lake, which had to be two or three acres in size, where the geese and ducks had gathered, and their weight pushed the ice down until it broke, and they had created a small pond in which they could paddle around, and get to the water to quench their thirst as they ate the food the tourists and villagers were feeding them. The day soon warmed up a bit, and it turned out to be a beautiful day for a walk. And walk I did.

I think I stayed in Reykjavik five days. The food was a little different, and it seemed like each meal was served with plenty of broccoli, which I really didn't care for, but it was okay with catsup, lots of catsup. The food was expensive, and I wasn't going to let much of it go to waste. The onion rings were good and crispy, and though I don't normally eat onion rings, I enjoyed these very much. What was really different was the steak I ordered a couple of times. I expected beef, but I don't think they had beef, but instead I think it was reindeer, or some other type of exotic animal. It was good, just not what I expected when I ordered steak. Breakfast was pretty normal, and I had cereal with fruit and milk most of the time. Other than this, I ate a few nutrition bars and some type of fruity soda, that was a bit unusual but good. Anyway, I didn't have any extreme gastric disturbances due to the food.

I headed home and was really sad about Hjordis (Jordie), but there is nothing I could have done about that. I had shed enough tears for her, and it was time to once again move forward. Another dip in my roller coaster ride, but I am strong and will cope. Ride the roller coaster, up and down and up and down. The saying is what goes up must come down. The good news is it never stays down, unless you let it. Never stay down.

The trip itself was a big adventure, and I really enjoyed that, and do not regret going to Iceland. I would go again in a heartbeat, but there are so many more places I want to visit too. Now that I have my passport to other international adventures, it is time to see more of the world.

Chapter 23
Traveling, Sumy and E.

It was easy to find women online, and pick and choose and maybe, just maybe, find that perfect woman for me. I talked to women from all over the world and had a lot of fun talking to and getting to know these women, most of whom were a little too young for me, but old farts like me like younger women and I am no different. I chatted with hundreds of women, and found a few hopefuls here and there. I found a couple gals in Ukraine I really liked. I found I had an affinity for Russian women, but after several trips to Ukraine, I did not get anywhere with the women there. Still, I enjoyed the traveling and seeing new countries and meeting new people, with few exceptions. Not everyone was who or what they appeared to be. There were those who were not interested in anything but scamming me. As time went on, it got easier to pick out those. As there are all kinds of people in the world, there were all kinds of women online, and you had better be careful with whom you talk, and especially what information you give them. I think the odds of finding the perfect woman is much better accomplished online, but just know that everyone will not be whom they appear to be.

 I made three trips to Sumy, Ukraine in all, and really enjoyed the trips. I first flew to Baltimore, Maryland, and then took a connecting flight to Paris, France. The French police were quite rude when I was searching for a restroom once, while I was passing through, but I wasn't there very long, so no big deal. Then, I took another connecting flight to Kiev, the capitol of Ukraine. Sumy was about a four-hour car trip to the east of the capitol city of Kiev, and I got to see a lot of the countryside getting to Sumy. During one trip, the giant sunflower plants were in full bloom, and there were acres and acres of big yellow flowers. There were a couple incidents, where there was a guy who had to pee along the roadway. There seemed to be very few restrooms along the way. Would these guys try to hide behind the vehicle? No! In fact, they seemed to be in a peeing contest, arching the stream at about 45 degrees to get the greatest distance out of the pee. I had a woman with me when one of these incidents occurred. We just looked at each other and smiled. I thought this was funny. I would usually stay in Sumy for ten to fourteen days at a time.

Kiev is a very large and beautiful city with a lot of huge churches adorned with gold. We visited one of these churches, and got a chance to go into the bell tower to look out over the city. The workings of the bell ringer were exposed, and this very old and intricate machine was quite fascinating. While in Ukraine, I spent some time in Kiev, and rode the subway for my first time ever. I walked the city, and meandered around in their underground mall under the streets of a central courtyard. With one of my new woman friends, I went to Kiev from Sumy via train, and this was my first time ever on a train too. There were so many sights to see, and I have photos of most of them. There were outdoor shops selling anything and everything. It was a good experience and I really enjoyed my time in Kiev, but it was mainly the company I was keeping that I enjoyed.

Most of the traveling within the cities was by foot. We took an occasional taxi when we had to go quite a distance, but for the most part we walked to everyday places within the city. We also took a boat trip while in Kiev, and dined on Russian beer and calamari. I noticed a very large wooden boat with no windows and it looked very strange. I was told it was going to be a restaurant when finished. It looked like Noah's ark. I didn't see any animals.

While in Kiev, the lady I was with wanted to go ice skating at a local rink. I had never been ice skating, but since I had roller skated when I was younger, I decided to give it a try. I didn't think ice skating would be so much different from roller skating, but I was wrong. Though I think I did pretty well for my first time and only fell three times, skating on ice was again a whole new experience. One fall was very bad, and I think I could have easily broken a leg. I did strain one knee badly and the pain was excruciating, but I never let on to my date how much it hurt. The pain would last for weeks, and I can still feel the damaged knee years later, but not enough to cause any real problems.

Most of my time was spent in Sumy, and I really loved this town. It was a compact city with a population of about a quarter million, but it didn't seem all that big. I know, as I walked all over most of it. One of the reasons I liked Sumy, was it had a river running through the middle of it. I spent a lot of time around this river. Sumy and Kiev were not clean like Iceland, but I didn't care. I was having fun. There were flowers everywhere, and the very old and beautiful buildings with their unique architecture made for a lot of good photos. There was also a carnival in the park, and we enjoyed a couple of the rides very much, especially the large Ferris wheel where I got a good bird's eye view of the city.

There were a lot of quaint restaurants, and I ate so many different kinds of food I had never eaten, like octopus. The shrimp, or prawn as they called them, were very tiny, just barely over an inch long when they were cooked or pickled, whatever the case may be, but they were so flavorful it was impossible to miss their taste in the meals we had. Sumy was basically a farming community, and this was evident everywhere, with all the fruits, vegetables and juices you would find in the restaurants and in their marketplace. One of my favorite places was their central market, where there were literally hundreds of shops arranged in a circular maze with a central meat market. You could literally buy anything you wanted in this shopping center. Jewelry, toiletries, baked goods, clothes, and leather goods were scattered in a random manner, as well as so much fresh produce it was at times difficult to find the right vegetable for a meal. There were some things I didn't recognize. The strange thing was you could find bread on one side of the walkway, and clothes on the other side, or a jewelry shop, next to a deli, next to a flower shop. There was no sense of organization, and this added to the beauty of the place. There were always plenty of fresh cut flowers to be found.

A noticeable sight was the "brick" buildings as I called them. They were apartment buildings which had probably been barracks at one time. They were huge drab concrete blocks, probably two or three apartments wide and maybe ten apartments long, and all nine stories high. They were concrete colored with no paint, and basically looked like huge concrete bricks. There were a dozen or more of these huge concrete blocks and they all looked the same. At least one of these apartments where I spent time was comfortable, cozy and very well decorated. Some were nicer than others. I guess it depended upon the woman.

One really cool thing happened one day when I was out alone. Much of the time while I was in Sumy, I was escorting someone around or visa versa. I did have some alone time though. One day I was getting a bit hungry, and I stopped at one of the vendor shops near the central market, where I saw a man cooking what looked like pork on a skewer. He sliced pork onto what looked like a tortilla, added lettuce and tomato and then something resembling mayonnaise. He rolled it up then seared it on a grill, to make something resembling a burrito. I could not speak much Russian on this trip, but was learning. As it turned out though, the vendor could speak French, and I had taken French in college. Think about this for a second, an American and Russian Ukrainian communicating in French. This cannot be an everyday occurrence. I ordered a burrito in broken French, and would see and talk to this vendor again, as the burrito was very good. It may not have been very good for the heart, as it was very greasy, but it tasted good. I could almost feel my arteries hardening after eating the very filling meal, but that was okay too. I would walk it off, as almost all my traveling was on foot. Occasionally I'd take a subway, train, taxi or boat, but most of my travel was on foot, even at night. This could have been a little dangerous alone at night, but I was a big strong guy and didn't think for a second I would be bothered, and I never was. The neighborhoods I walked in at night seemed to be some of the better neighborhoods in the city.

I was in Sumy in late fall, early spring, and early summer on different trips, and the seasons were quite different. There was a frost or two with light freezes at night a few times, but most of the weather while I was there was very pleasant. I even wore shorts and short sleeves much of the time, even though I carried a jacket. There was no snow while I was there. Picnics were a big to do while I was there, and I enjoyed those very much. We had picnics along the river and in the forest. The forest had a lot of pine and birch trees, and it smelled fresh, especially after breathing the air in the not so clean city. Geese were flying around a nearby lake, and the sounds of nature were everywhere. We went hunting for mushrooms once, but there were not many mushrooms to be found. Most of the mushrooms we did find were poisonous. They said the weather had been too dry, and mushrooms do not grow when the weather is dry, but wandering around in the cool of the forest was pleasant nevertheless. We cooked fresh fish over an open fire, and had a good time. The food was delicious, as was the company. These are memories I will carry with me forever.

The form of currency in Ukraine is the hryvnia, pronounced griev-na, and I thought it was fun learning to handle and dispense a foreign currency. The exchange rate was eight to one US dollar. I had learned to count in Russian, which also helped a bit, though I was not very good at it. An old lady selling flowers did not seem to pronounce the words quite like the ladies I was escorting. Learning the Russian language is really tough, since they do not have the same alphabet as we do. They have more letters, as well as a couple accent letter groups. To give you an example of how difficult it was, they have a letter that looks like a 'p', but it is pronounced like an 'r'. They have many letters which do not resemble our letters at all. A letter that looks like a 'y' is pronounced like our double 'oo'. I have however learned numerous words and phrases, and continue to work on the language from time to time. I doubt I will ever get fluent in the language.

It was not just the women I was enjoying, though I was enjoying them very much. It was also the country and the new sights and new experiences which made the trips pleasant. I found a place serving steak, as I am a meat and potato lover, but I'm not really sure what animal the steak was from. I ate a lot of vegetables, and even learned to like a few of them. I found I really liked calamari or squid, though I had eaten squid a few times before. It just seemed so much better there than when I had previously eaten it. Most of the food was very good. One thing I liked very much was halva. The pulp left after sunflower seeds are pressed for their oil, was sweetened and packaged into small bricks. It was a very delicious treat. I ate borscht, which is a beet soup. I really didn't care for it much, but as it is the Russian national soup, I ate it anyway. One of the gals I was seeing made some homemade borscht for me, and it was much better than the soup served in restaurants, but not really something I would care to eat every day.

There were many restaurants which were not only new eating experiences, but very entertaining as well. One appeared to be a dungeon, and the entrance led us down a stairway to the basement of the building. The walls were adorned with chainmail, knight's armor and all sorts of ancient weapons. The atmosphere was romantic, and the hostess was dressed the part of a seductive wench. One restaurant had belly dancers, and this was very stimulating. There was live music, and the belly dancers would come around to our table and put on a show for tips. Another restaurant was actually a sailing ship. We ate on the stern of the boat in the open air, and the crisp and cool clear night was lit by lanterns. This was a romantic setting for a dinner date, especially since the lady I was escorting was a little underdressed for the cool night. This made for a very close and cozy night. The meal was good too.

As I was traveling quite a bit and staying gone for weeks at a time, I was not able to take good care of my cattle. Flooding for a couple years was making it even more difficult to take care of my cattle, my pets, so I decided to sell them. Cattle prices were high at the time, and I got a bundle of cash for them, which helped fund all the traveling I was doing. Once again I was out of the cattle business. I did miss them for a while, as I had grown quite fond of them. They were not just cattle, but my pets, and gave me a lot of personal satisfaction, but times change and things change.

I continued my online search for that one special woman who could be my partner for the rest of my life. I met a lot of women, mostly too young for me, but continued nevertheless. I met a lot of really nice women, but none who were really just right for me, and who satisfied all my many criteria for the perfect woman. Then, finally on January 10, 2009 I met a gal who appeared to be really good for me. She was very nice, good looking, very smart and younger than me, but not that many years younger, and she was of Russian descent. But she wasn't living in Russia, Ukraine, or some other Russian speaking country. She lived in Texas less than 150 miles from me. She was born and went to school in New York City, and moved to California after she got out of high school and spent most of her adult life in California, until she moved to Austin, TX around 2005. Austin is where we met and had a pleasant lunch, then a walk along Lady Bird Lake. We liked each other enough to meet again.

I literally looked at thousands of women from all over the world, and to think I would find the perfect woman this close to where I lived never crossed my mind, but it happened. Turns out she is not perfect, but seems to be close enough. She even satisfied some criteria I had not previously considered. Technically there is no perfect woman, but we see eye to eye on so many things, she is much closer to being Ms. Perfect for me than anyone I have met so far. Ellen is so close in fact I have quit looking for someone better, and for good reason. We travel and have a lot of fun together, and I am happier than I believe I have ever been. Pretty darn close anyway.

After a couple years of being single since my divorce, I found I enjoy my life and my freedom and I really didn't want to get married again, not even to the right woman whom I eventually found. I think I can be happier not married, and have decided I will stay single for the rest of my life, which is my choice and my right. I can do what I want when I want, and am determined to stay single, even now that I have that very special woman in my life, I did eventually find, after a very long search process. Ellen may want to get married eventually, but not at the present. We have compromised on this issue with a commitment and companion ring from me. It seems like we have very few real issues, and we are able to resolve these issues quickly. There seems to be nothing else to interfere with our happiness.

There will always be people who will try to get you to do things you really don't want to do. These people may be loved ones, family, or even people you do not know, and these people will always be out there. They will try to change you, and what you have planned to do with your life. I know what I want to do, and even though I had to compromise with Ellen to keep her happy, this was something I really wanted to do, should have done, and finally did after nearly three years together. Don't let people talk you into things you really don't want to do, or into things that will interfere with your happiness. I currently think being single will keep me happy and am committed to staying single. There will always be a need to compromise in life, and you may lose a little freedom in making compromises, but nothing really changed for me with Ellen. I think the commitment ring actually improved our relationship. And I kept my freedom. You should have the strength to do what will keep you happy with your life too, and if it helps make someone else happy, then that's all the better. I can't teach you this, but I can tell you to watch for the pitfalls which can and will entangle and strangle your life. Think before you act, and act according to your feelings and desires, not the feelings and desires of someone else. I thought the commitment ring over for a couple months before I actually gave it to her, and we had a lovely ceremony at one of our favorite restaurants which made it even more special and memorable.

Test time again!

If you are driving your boat and facing forward, which side is the port side?

1. Right side
2. Left side
3. Rear

Answer on page 124

Why do shrimp and crab shed their skin or shell?

1. They just want a shiny new skin or shell
2. It's is the way they clean themselves
3. Their skin or shell does not grow
4. They can only mate when they remove their skin or shell and are soft

Answer on page 133

What was the worst setback I had in building my home?

1. Lack of money
2. Too much company business
3. Hurt back
4. Hurt leg

Answer on page 155

All the questions in this book are intentionally easy, and none are to try to trick you. They are simply to test to see if you are remembering what you are reading. If you are having trouble with the questions, you may need to seek professional help.

Church in Kiev, Ukraine

Chapter 24
Las Vegas

Traveling is still big in my life, and Ellen's life. We have been to Baja, Mexico and quite a few states in the US visiting her sister, brother and parents, but also having some fun in Las Vegas and other trips just for the fun of it. So far we have enjoyed trips to California, Colorado, Florida, Mississippi, Tennessee, Washington state and D.C. We have traveled to some of these places several times. We will always have a trip or two in the works, and plan to travel as much as we can. A trip to Curacao is currently booked.

Ellen does not play poker, but she has no problem with me playing all I want or need. In fact, she supports my poker, as she has learned I am not going to throw my life away playing the game. I like to play and will travel and play, but I do not let the game rule my life. I will be financially responsible, and play to only the extent I can afford. I continue to play in the World Series of Poker, and this, my fourth year playing in the greatest game on Earth I managed to place in the money. This was the largest Senior Event ever, with over 3,700 entrants. I finished at 217th place with 396 places paid, so I placed fairly high in the money. I got busted out when I flopped a straight, and the guy across the table who was also in the hand, pushed all in as he thought he had the best hand. He didn't, but sucked out on the river card, making a bigger straight to beat me. It was a tough beat, but that's poker!

Poker has helped me mellow out a bit. With all the bad cards, the tough beats and some pretty bad beats, which are inevitable and come along regularly, one learns to accept this is how it is, and always will be, with life and poker. I have not had a true bad beat though, which is a monster hand beat by another and bigger monster hand. By a monster hand I mean quads (four of a kind), or a straight flush (a five card straight, all cards in the same suit; hearts, clubs, spades, or diamonds). This is so rare, many casinos have bad beat jackpots which pay those involved, should this happen in a cash game, but not in the tournaments. Bad beats are rare, but they do happen, just not to me yet, but I'm certain if I play long enough, it could eventually happen to me. I have had quads many times, and they have always won. I don't recall having a straight flush in a live game, but have had this hand a couple times online.

The best possible hand is a royal flush, an ace high straight flush. I have had one of these in my life, online. Online poker plays at a faster rate than live poker, as the hands are shuffled by computer rather than by a real dealer. Online, the cards are shuffled and dealt almost instantly, and you can play usually up to two or three hands a minute, especially if the table is not full of players. A full poker table plays nine or ten players. I have occasionally played at live poker tables with eleven players, when a casino was trying to get the maximum number of players in a tournament, and they didn't have enough tables for everyone to play at a standard ten player table. The more people there are at a table, the more difficult it is to win a hand.

As I was saying, poker has helped me mellow out a bit, as you must learn patience and keep your emotions out of the game. There can be a lot of emotion in a poker game and I see some of this emotion regularly, but you better be able to keep it under control or you will not win many poker games. Having a good poker face and keeping your emotions totally in check can be critical in bigger games, with the best players in the world you will find playing in the World Series of Poker. There are so many people in the world who play poker, and are highly emotional and do not control their emotions, walk around with a chip on their shoulders and get mad easily, and for the most part, do not care if they act like assholes. These people shouldn't be playing at a poker table, but they do. You see them at the cash tables and smaller tournaments, but you generally do not see them in the bigger games like the World Series. That is one reason I like playing in the World Series.

When a player gets upset and begins to play foolishly, it is said he is on "tilt". A player on tilt usually does not last long in a tournament, or loses all his money in a cash game. This is not a good way to play poker. Emotions must be controlled.

You have to really feel sorry for these poor players, as they seem to be pissed off most of the time. Some people will never be good poker players, and when they try they seem to stay pissed because they couldn't handle getting beat, playing what they think are good hands, but in fact are mediocre hands they play because they just think they are naturally lucky, and are supposed to win all the time. Believe me, these people are out there playing, and are really miserable people to be around, but if you play smart you can take advantage of them, which is also part of the game.

There are always a few unpleasant people at the poker tables anyway, but as a rule, the better and bigger the tournament, the more control the players have. This year at the Senior World Series of Poker Event, there was only one player I can recall who was really an ass, and this is out of over 3,700 people. He had two things against him, he was drinking too much and he was a lawyer. That is two strikes against him in my book, and I'm sure in many people's book. While he was really lucky for a while, the cards eventually turned against him, and playing like a moron got him busted out of the tournament. Good riddance!

If you spend enough time in poker rooms, you will see some pretty strange things. Spending time in poker rooms also means spending a lot of time in restrooms, as at every break everyone heads to the restroom first off. I was at the urinals once, and I don't want to knock this guy too much, because he was apparently well-hung and trying to get the last drop of pee off his pecker, and really doing a lot of shaking at the urinal next to me. I'm just glad there was a divider between us, because I thought this guy was trying to rope a calf with his apparently healthy lasso. Enough said!

There was this one gal playing at a cash table in Caesar's Palace one night, and I was sitting across from her, but before

I get to her, I would like to explain the seating arrangements at a poker table. A dealer sits in the middle of one side of the table and deals the cards. The first seat to his left is seat one at the table. Seat two is clockwise around the table, all the way around the table to seat ten, just to the dealer's right. Well, this gal, a school teacher from Montana, and a very nice and well-endowed teacher at that, was sitting in seat ten in her low cut dress. I was sitting in seat six facing her slightly to my left. Well, this gal was sitting with her arms crossed on the poker table railing, and every time the dealer would place cards on the table, this gal would lean forward pressing her breasts against her arms, thus squeezing her breasts to the point where they seemed to be very near to the point where they were going to pop out of her dress. She would do this, every time the dealer would place cards on the table, and everyone at the table was getting a good look at her jewels. We couldn't help but notice and I would look as well, and maybe I had begun to drool, as finally she looked up at me and said "are you staring at my boobs?" Without hesitation, I said "if you are going to keep showing them to me, then I'm going to keep looking". Everyone laughed, including her with a big smile. She kept up the boobie press, and the friendly talk continued at the table, but then she ended up playing a hand against me. We would both flop top pair of queens, but I had a better kicker. Everyone at the table appeared to be mad at me when I took all her money, and busted her out, no pun intended, and she left the table. When playing a poker hand, you play the best five cards of the seven you have to play, with the two in your hand plus the five community cards. Sometimes, as with the one pair (the same pair) we each had, a higher card in your hand will also play when there are smaller cards on the table. The high card in your hand is your kicker.

During my earlier trips to Las Vegas, I took a lot of photos and a few videos with the camera I always took with me on my travels. There is so much to see in Las Vegas, so I take photos every time I go. I got a bigger memory chip for my camera so I could take more photos and videos, without having to transfer them to my computer as often. I have also burned a lot of batteries along the way. I still continue to take a few photos, but have already taken enough of Las Vegas. I really love to take pictures, and always keep a photo and video record of my travels. One day I may not be able to travel, and I will have a big hoard of memories in the form of photos and video clips I use to make movies with the help of a computer movie program. I also burn some DVD's of these movies, so I will not lose my memories should I have a computer failure.

One such unforgettable memory was created when I was playing in a cash game at Caesar's Palace one evening. This attractive gal walked up to the table where her boyfriend was playing, and wanted him to quit and go play with her. She was bored with playing poker, and wanted to go do something else. Her boyfriend just wanted to play poker, and refused her requests. I told her I would go play with her, and she said okay. I went and cashed out my poker chips, and we left the poker room. She wanted to play craps, but the tables were full and there was no room for us. We ended up playing the slots. I put a hundred dollars in each of our slots, and we sat for nearly an hour and enjoyed each other's company. I know I certainly enjoyed hers. I broke even, and she even won a little money. We cashed out, and I took my hundred back and gave her the winnings. We then went to dinner. After our date, I took her back to her boyfriend who was still at the poker table. After this, I would see the couple several more times, and her boyfriend seemed to pay a little more attention to his girlfriend.

Chapter 25
Overcrowding and Space

I talked a little earlier about me having the space to run wild when I was younger, and to some extent I still have a good deal of personal space to do what I want and need to do. But much of this space has dwindled away. There are a lot more people in the area, and I can feel the effects of overcrowding. Humans are just one of the many animal species on this planet. We are probably the most dangerous and most vicious of all animals. When we live too close together, we will fight and kill each other at worst, and at best will agitate, annoy and irritate each other. If you do not have your space, other people will constantly annoy you, and you cannot be truly happy. Also, if it should become necessary for your property to provide all you need to survive, a single city lot cannot do this. How much space do you need to provide a constant source of meat, veggies, fruit, and most importantly water, for all your needs? You must have enough space to provide these needs. Remember too, all your neighbors will also have the same needs, and you will be in direct competition with them for the available resources. I could not live in a city, and will not live in the city. There are just too many people, and I cannot live that way. In addition, if forced to survive, there will be much competition and only the strongest will survive. I guess city people can't miss what they have never had. But many do know what it's like outside the city, in the mountains, camping, skiing, wide open spaces and exotic vacations. These people live in the city, but yearn to be out of the city, and alone. There is a reason for this. They do not have enough elbow room. I suppose as long as others continue to supply them with food and water, city parks and golf courses may suffice for some, but it is not the same as having your own space.

    I really like Las Vegas, where most of the time, it is really crowded. But this is another type of crowding, as it is just temporary for me. People are there to have fun, and for the most part, they are having fun and not annoying each other. Even though it is crowded, people are paying attention to the sights and sounds of the city, their friends, and their business, and are generally not interested in those around them. But when they go back home, probably a quite a few of these people go back to being very annoying.

The World Series of Poker rooms at the Rio get very crowded, and you have to literally wade through people to get where you want to go, but these are some of the better people around. They have little or no thought of irritating others. They are there to have fun, and that is what they are doing. In four years, I have not seen a single fight in Las Vegas, or any casino for that matter. Considering the number of people, I think this is rare and a testament to these people. These are smarter people than you will find on average, on the streets of your typical city or town. You go back to your city or town, people will irritate and annoy each other, and some will do so to the point of fighting. People in general are not all that smart. They are rude, arrogant, belligerent, combative, self-centered, egotistical assholes to one extent or another. Hell, even I have a little of every one of these common traits. I'm not perfect either. I am just in a little more control of my emotions than your average person, and this is partly due to poker.

Stay out of other people's affairs. You have enough problems, without getting into someone else's problems. It seems there are way too many people who want to control other people, and tell them what they can and cannot do. This is especially true with government. Government is run by power hungry individuals who weasel their way into office in a November popularity contest. They then churn out further restrictions which prevent people from doing things they think are immoral or just plain wrong, according to their upbringing. Take for example, gambling in Texas. Texas does not allow casinos here. No one has the right to tell me what I can and cannot do with my own money. But Texas does. They say I cannot gamble in a casino in Texas, but they sell lottery tickets and scratch offs by the billions. The hypocrites! Uppity busybodies who have no life of their own, and just aren't content unless they can screw with someone else's life. What they are doing is just plain wrong. Government is way too intrusive in our lives, and this has got to stop. That is not likely to happen anytime soon though, so the best you can do is to try to keep to your own space away from these hypocrites.

Space is measured in acres, not in feet, as in your home or apartment. Your backyard is not enough space unless you have a very large backyard as I do, but at times my backyard is just not enough. Your space has to be measured in acres, and the more acres, the better. If you do not have your space, you need to find it either locally or somewhere else, but whatever you do, find your space. As the population continues to grow, it will reach the point one day, where no one can find their space.

Assume for a minute you, and everyone around you, must each provide for your every need, with no outside help. How far do you need to go to find water? There is no water company, and your faucets do not work. How far do you need to go to find meat, fruit, and vegetables? The grocery stores are empty. How about firewood, to cook your food and heat your home in the winter? There is no electricity and no gas. I will assume for a second you have shelter, and not need to provide this for now, but in reality, you may need to do this too. Look around you. How much space do you need to provide your food and water? More than you have would be my guess. Everywhere you look, you see other people who are also looking for food and water. Is there enough for all of you? If you live in a city, most of you will starve to death. Do you still think you have enough space? Maybe you do now, but what about tomorrow? Do you realize how dependent your life is upon others? What is their competency to do this? Something to think about, don't you think?

Space is the reason I am a big advocate for population control. Our population is out of control. As our population grows, people are thrust closer and closer together. As this happens, the inevitability of people to annoy, irritate and aggravate each other increases, and the result will be devastating for some. Yet, people continue to immigrate to the US, and we allow this. People continue to have babies, who have no business having babies, and people invade our borders, and we do too little about this. One of the problems is government sees more people as more taxpayers. The truth is these baby makers and invaders have historically become more of a drain to our government and natural resources. If you already have several babies, you have no business having any more. If you cannot afford to have a baby financially, you have no business having a baby. These fetuses should be immediately terminated. Why can't someone do something about this? Why can't we keep the invaders out?

Doctors shouldn't be saving people who have no chance of a normal life. This is just plain stupid, and if you are one of the doctors doing this, you are a MORON! Expensive medicines, procedures and surgeries! You're doing this for whom? For you and the pill pushers! If you are doing this for old folks, you are also taking advantage of the Medicare system and making a lot of extra money, but you are still a moron. A deformed or retarded baby should not be allowed into this world, with today's testing methods. Accidentally maybe; but intentionally, no! Partial infants, with no chance of a normal life, can only be a drain to the finances and sanity of their parents, and the government, at times forced to support these non-productive people. There are too many bleeding hearts who think <u>all</u> life is precious. This is not true. Life as a vegetable is no life at all, and termination of these lives is the only logical thing to do, and the only humane thing to do. Wildlife on the other hand, is precious and will become more so as time goes on, and as humans expand and crowd. If life were rare, then that life might be precious, but human life is not rare. Human life is at the other extreme, and more must die than are currently dying, or we will choke our planet to death. You can tune the television to the news every day, and see people dying and others saying how sad it is. I say more room for me, you and those who need the space left behind by those who die. This world would be a much better place to live if suddenly a couple billion people would disappear from the face of the planet.

People have babies in some cases, because they can get more from government in the form of aid, which they use to improve their lives, not the lives of their babies. This is just plain wrong, and there should be some form of punishment for this, and the babies terminated. Others have babies because they are just too stupid to keep their legs together or their pecker in their pants. This is stupid and wrong too. Abortion is one solution, and rigid birth control should be mandatory in many cases. Sterilization is another tool that will remedy a lot of problems. Sterilization is not a cruel and inhumane punishment as some think. I am sterile and have been for many years. I think being sterile is great, and the reason is condoms are not needed, except for disease control. Sterility can result in much greater sexual satisfaction, and there are not too many things I would trade this for. Sterility, however, does not give someone the sexual freedom to take what is not given freely. Rape is still a crime, and violators should be severely punished, even more so than they are now. This applies to both men and women, or as it happens in way too many cases, with children. Sex with a minor is rape. If you also happen to be a minor, you should be punished. If you happen to be an adult, you should be executed. All fetuses resulting from rape should be terminated.

Some people should not even be allowed to reproduce, as every time they do, the gene pool suffers miserably. If you do not smarten up a little, you may be a good candidate for sterilization, at least in my book. This should give you a little something to think about, as you try to learn a little from my book. I want you to become smarter. Do you want to be smarter? Or, do you promote dumb people? It is illogical to punish people for being ignorant, but government says ignorance of the law is no excuse. Then why does government promote dumb people?

Immigration should end immediately, and this can and should be ended <u>now</u>! We do not need more citizens, and especially non-citizens, in our country. In many cases, those wanting to come over here, only want to come here to escape the miserable conditions in their own country, and a bunch of idiots over here, just keep letting them come here. They should stay home, and fight and sacrifice with their neighbors, to try to achieve a better life. Some do, but <u>all</u> should. At least these days, there are some countries where the people are fighting for the rights and privileges all people should have. It just seems they are isolated incidents, and not really enough.

Our forefathers fought and died for what we have. The people in other countries should do the same, if they ever hope to have what we have for themselves, or their children. These people immigrate to our country, legally and illegally, and our country allowing them to do so, makes the fight for rights in their home country more difficult for those who stay behind. I can understand they do not want to die; that they want to live a better life, but it is my opinion they are cowards. They are selfish and are only concerned for themselves. Others are nothing more than thieves and thugs. This can be very irritating, and not good for our society. Any country in the world can have what we have; they don't need to come over here to get it. All they need to do is organize and fight for their rights and independence. This is easier said than done, but necessary. Americans have pride in their country, even with all the problems we have, because our country was built with blood, sweat, and tears. It may take years or decades to accomplish, but that is, or at least should be, their destiny, not running away like cowards. Keep it up, and what we have may one day not be worth coming over here for. We are certainly headed in that direction. Maybe some of our bleeding hearts, who allow these immigrants into our country, should go to their countries to join the fight. Ha! That's not going to happen.

Natural disasters such as hurricanes, tornadoes, floods,

earthquakes, and non-natural disasters such as the 911 World Trade Center and Pentagon disasters among others, have involved more than just a few people in the past decade (ten years) or so, and have been worse because of the enormous number of people who have congregated into very tight areas. These people did not have their space, and they were packed together like sardines. The more people are spread out and the more space between people, the less damage when disaster strikes. Overcrowding makes disasters worse. As our population continues to grow denser, the number of deaths from disasters in overcrowded areas will increase. It seems these disasters can't kill enough people though, to make a big enough impact on the swelling population. You can't put too many people in a given area, and not expect problems.

Currently in the US, disasters cause a lot of pain and suffering for those directly involved in the disasters, but thanks to our government, the rest of us also feel your pain. These disasters, which seem fairly large, are just a drop in the bucket to what can and must happen, to reduce our population. And our bleeding hearts in government seem to feel they have to help all these people recover from these disasters, thus f_#%ing up our economy and hurting the rest of us. Keep throwing $billions around like it is nothing, and our economy will never recover. Keep pumping millions of gallons of oil into the Gulf of Mexico and the oceans, not to mention the tons and tons of toxic chemicals released into the air every day, damaging large quantities of our natural resources, and the money may not matter in the long term. But for the short term, stop throwing money away! It is not yours to give away. If you really need to throw the money away, throw some my way. I could use a little more. You just never know what is going to happen. The money may <u>really</u> be needed someday, and there will be none. We will have given it all away. Maybe we should save a little for later. I guess you can't really save what you don't have! We are in hock up to our ears, and nothing is really ours anymore.

Something really bad can and will happen, if not tomorrow,

then maybe the next day. Can rampant disease or famine from overcrowding be in our future? When will Earth be again impacted by a huge asteroid? The handwriting is on the wall, and this is just a plain and simple fact that cannot be denied. The laws of probability say that while the likelihood of a global killer asteroid may be very small, sooner or later some serious shit is going to happen. Population reduction will happen. I may not see it in my lifetime, but it is inevitable. By the time this planet sees another devastating asteroid will Earth already be a dead planet from our pollution, or possibly a nuclear war? There are many possibilities. Will it be a disaster we could have avoided, or will it be from something from way out in left field? We need to be optimistic, right? Yes, but we must also not press our luck, by not dealing with problems we can solve right now.

Overcrowding cannot and should not be allowed to continue. Take the example of the pasture I was raising my cattle on. I had about a dozen head, plus calves, on about 25 acres of pasture land. I could have made a lot more money if I had instead put fifty head of cattle on this land, right? Wrong! Fifty head of cattle could not have been sustained on the acreage, as there were not enough natural resources (grass) to sustain this number of cattle. It would not be practical to try to raise fifty head of cattle on this plot of land, as they need a certain amount of space, and the same is true for the number of people who currently populate the United States and the world. Just how smart do you have to be to realize this? Or do you just not give a damn? Well, someone had better start giving a damn. There were no serious disasters to strike my cattle, but if I had fifty head of cattle, the probability of a severe disaster occurring to them would have been much greater. They would have mostly starved to death. I know this, and you should know this as well.

Huge population concentrations insure huge population destruction, and therefore population reduction. Sparse rural population insures protection from extinction. When disaster strikes in cities, and this is entirely random, a lot of people will die. If the same disaster strikes a rural area, sure some people will die, but because they were scattered here and there, a lot less will die. City folk will be clueless about how to survive, how to find food and water, and most will die, millions of them. You think this is cold and cruel? Maybe so, but this is certainly something that needs saying. Do I cry when someone dies? Hell no, and you are not going to cry when I die. I would never expect you to cry for me. I will have just made a little more space for you. You need your space to live. You can survive maybe, but you cannot <u>live</u> without adequate space. I want to live; how about you?

Chapter 26
Religion

If you are pissed off at me now, then you are going to be really pissed off by the time you get finished with this chapter. It is said you don't talk religion or politics with friends. The reason is when you do talk about religion or politics; you will no longer have your friends. Well, we are not friends, and I AM going to talk about religion now and politics a little later. Jesus, the son of God, was born and died 2,000 years ago amongst slaves, and the most backward and ignorant people on this planet. I don't know what he said or did to create such a huge following amongst these backward people, but I'll give him credit for that. But now we are no longer an ignorant or backward people, or are we? Don't get me wrong though, I do believe in God, and I believe in the tooth fairy, gremlins, ghosts and goblins, the Devil, and witches, but they only exist in the minds of people. They do exist because people want them to exist, and they exist in the minds of a lot of people, but to think they are real is absurd. We are in the midst of a very severe drought here in Texas, and people have been praying to God and Jesus for rain. Were their prayers answered, and did it rain? In some cases, it did, but not because of their prayers. It rained because the climatic conditions existed for the rain to fall, which was produced by low pressure, high pressure, evaporation of water by the sun, and the natural movements of the earth, not because God made it rain.

People think God or Jesus is going to save them financially or keep them from harm, when the fact is only hard work and financial planning will help you. If God can help keep you from harm, then he can also maim and kill. Thousands and tens of thousands of people are killed and maimed every day. Innocent little babies die every day, not having lived long enough to give a loving God reason for Him to kill them. If there is a real God, He is a mass murderer and a really cruel son-of-a-bitch. You may say the Devil did this, but if your God is all knowing and all powerful, your God would not, and could not, let the Devil kill.

Then you have the religious fanatics who use God as an excuse to maim and murder. These are some really sick bastards, but the end result is they are reducing the planetary population. War does the same thing, and pissed off sons-of-bitches killing the sick bastards, and them killing back is good for the planet overall. This slows down our self-destruction by reducing the population which is destroying the resources we need to survive. There is a silver lining behind every act of destruction. Now I don't condone war and terrorist acts that maim and kill people, because war and terrorism are not the way to save our planet and will never ultimately save our planet, but for the current time, is one of the most effective sources of population reduction.

If you believe in God, then why is God causing earthquakes and famines, that are destroying billions of dollars' worth of property and killing so many people? How about tsunamis? Does God create those too? If you believe in God, he does. Like I said, if you choose to believe in God, then you have to also believe he is a cruel, mass murdering son-of-a-bitch. This planet cannot move forward into a more modern society, as long as it retains the religious and backward beliefs produced 2,000 years ago by a really ignorant and backward primitive people. To choose to remain ignorant and backward is not logical. You have the opportunity to learn, and you should do so. You have the opportunity to work hard and carve out a place for yourself on this planet, and you should do so. You have the opportunity to stand up on your own two feet, and make a happy and rewarding life for yourself. You don't need the crutch of a fictitious God. Or are you so ignorant and backward that you do? You have only one chance at life. Why wouldn't you try to make it the best it can be?

I hope I really pissed you off; this was my intention. Did I piss you off enough for you to think about your life, where you are at, and where you are headed? I certainly hope so. This can be a really great world where everyone is happy, satisfied with where they are at, and really and truly looking forward to the next day. What are you looking forward to now? Thinking God is going to make everything alright for you is not going to cut it; thinking God is going to give you all the money you need is not going to cut it; thinking God is waiting in Heaven to reward you for being a lazy, ignorant and backward son-of-a-bitch is not going to happen. You are eventually going to die, and you will decompose just like the armadillo, opossum or raccoon that got run over on the highway last night. You will rot and all you will be is fertilizer for a tree that might someday grow where you are planted in the ground. Using God as a crutch to help ease your pain is fine with me, but the end result will be the same. What really matters is not what happens after you die, what really matters is what happens when you live, and if you are not living, you may as well be dead. I choose to live, and this is exactly what I will do until the day I die, and when I die I will have lived a life worth living, and will have no regrets about dying, as I will have lived to the best of my ability.

I hear a lot about depressed people, and I think I know why so many people are depressed. They take pills for their depression, but pills are not what they need. What they need is a life. When you sit around all the time doing nothing, then I would expect this is enough reason for you to become depressed. I get a little idle from time to time, and I can sometimes feel a little depression coming over me, but I don't stay idle long. I start doing things. I get outside and do a little work. I go somewhere and have some fun. I write a book. Keeping busy is the best cure there is for depression. Do something constructive and keep at it for a few days, and I'll bet you, you will become less depressed. If working endless hours at a dead end job is what is making you depressed, then don't work so much. Have some fun doing whatever it is you like to do. If the job itself is what is depressing you, then change your job. You don't have to live with depression. You just need to get busy at living a balanced life, balanced between work and play. You don't need pills. Pills are never a long term solution. And remember, you are what you eat. Is your diet screwing up your body chemistry and thus making you depressed?

Up to now I have not lived fully 100% of the time, but I would not change a single thing in my life, because every experience has made me the person I am, and I think I am great. You may think I'm a psycho, a crazy son-of-a bitch, or just plain nuts, and you have the right to think as you do, but I AM great. Can you say the same? If not, then do something about it. Be smarter, be stronger, be happy and live life to its fullest, and when you die you will have no regrets. I have not always lived my life to the fullest, but I am now living as though there is no tomorrow. There really may be no tomorrow, and if life ends for me tomorrow, well, then that's life isn't it? I do not expect the world to listen to me, and the perfect world may be decades or even centuries away, if ever. But the sooner we get started, the sooner we will get there. Get started now; live; just do it!

Chapter 27
Politics

A good rule of thumb is you don't talk politics with friends if you want to keep your friends, but again we are not friends and are not likely to ever be friends, so I can also talk to you about politics. There is a good chance you are pretty pissed off by now after the last couple chapters, so you should probably take a couple aspirins and relax a bit, before taking on this next chapter. Let your blood pressure go back down. So, if you are really pissed off at me, and what I have been saying, and think you are about to explode, take a break right now and cool off a bit.

Now, that you are back and cooled off a bit, I'm going to talk about politics in the US, but also about some politics of the world too. We do not have the best political system in the world, though some would disagree. The problem with our system is not the system itself, the problem is there is just too much of it, trying to do too much for the lazy bastards out there who are too lazy to do for themselves, and doing a half-ass job of ridding society of the scum who would rob, plunder and destroy others. Too many rob or plunder over and over again. There is no excuse for this. If you get rid of all the criminals though, a lot of people would be out of a job, and government knows this. The problem is we fight too many wars that should be fought by others. We are not, and should not be the world's keeper. And the problem is we seem to need more oil than we can produce. We don't need such a huge government, when there are not enough workers in the private sector to financially support it. There are a lot of hard working people in the US, but not enough to support the financial needs of the government, so it taxes us at higher and higher rates. Our tax <u>rate</u> should never increase. If the government wants more money, it should insure its citizens always remain productive, earning a good living. Double our income, and government gets twice the money for its needs; cut our income in half, and they get half as much. You can't cut our incomes, and then take more. We do not have more to give, but our government is taking anyway. Most of the private sector does not have the resources to support our government, which always thinks it needs more, and will take it whether or not we have it to give. We have needs too. You can't take what we need to live. That is just too much government. Then there are the rich bastards who have their lawyers to find loopholes, so they can keep more of what they have, and the rich get richer and the poor get poorer. But who pays most of the taxes? Of course, those who can least afford to do so. What we really need is less government, but does anyone out there think this is going to happen? If you do, you are delusional.

If there be one person out there who thinks I am rich or wealthy, I am going to squash this thought right here and now. I have some land, but I am a poor SOB. I live below the poverty level, according to the government department which sets this standard, but I don't need much. I have no mortgage, I have no truck payment, my utilities are very low, and I just don't spend all that much. No more than I have, that is certain. And I have a budget! I cut and burn wood to heat my home, and probably the biggest single expense is fuel for my truck. Just because I am writing a book, does not make me wealthy. I am retired or at least semi-retired, as I do work a little, but I do not make a lot of money. Maybe this book will change this, as there are really are a lot of you folks out there who can really use my book. If nothing else, you can use it to start your fire in your fireplace for a while.

There are too many people in the US, and as time goes on and the population grows, so does the number of really dumb, idiotic, and just plain stupid people. I trust you are not one of these, as the really dumb, idiotic, and stupid people will not be capable of reading this book. Then you have the bleeding hearts who want to help these dumb people who are too lazy to learn the needed skills to succeed. Whatever happened to one of the main natural laws, survival of the fittest? It seems there are too many people who fall into this group of bleeding hearts, who want to save everyone, and at the same time process their hidden agenda of converting them to their religion. Many become dependent upon receiving help, instead of learning skills to help themselves. How many of these bleeding hearts work in and for our government? I know we certainly have plenty in the private sector, mostly affiliated with a religious group, but I bet there are many more affiliated with government, or get some benefit from government. But I am on politics, so let's get back to the subject of politics.

If you don't belong to a political action group of some sort, voting is a waste of time. You have no voice in government with only one vote. This is why I quit voting a long time ago. The people I was trying to get elected were always losing, so why vote? It seems the majority of people have a different view than I do, and I think therein lies a major problem with society today. If you are in this majority, you are one of the people who have f_#%ed up our government and our economy. I was consistently out voted. How about you? These days, I can't really see anyone deserving of my vote.

Even if you did have a little clout with your vote, you couldn't change government anyway. Government has gotten so huge, this monster can only be changed by allowing it to destroy itself from within, which lately it is doing a pretty good job of doing. Don't waste your time trying to change what you cannot change. And you can't fight government either. All you can do is to try to avoid it the best you can. There is a law against almost everything. Government has learned it can create jobs by creating criminals, and it can earn revenue by creating an endless supply of misdemeanor crimes, which they can charge you with, and make you pay fines for. This has become big business for our government. These days you couldn't get away with some of the stuff cousin Steve and I did when we were younger like trespassing, underage drinking, and drinking and driving, which by the way, I never do anymore. We didn't have the law enforcement we have today and didn't need it. We slept with our doors unlocked. You need to know the difference between the things you can change and the things you cannot change, and work on only the things you can change. There is not much you can change you will find, but the things you can change are mostly changed by hard work at your job and in your home domain. Remember hard work never killed anyone. Well, maybe, but that's the saying. It nearly killed me, but the hard work also made me tough enough to withstand the bomb that went off in my lap.

I have thought of running for political office a time or two, but didn't feel I had enough popularity to do any good, and besides, I also didn't think I could kiss enough asses to get elected. Maybe kick some ass, but kiss? No! I am not a good enough liar to get elected either, and my public speaking abilities are not good. I can write what I want to say alright, but by the time this book is finished, it will have been written and re-written several times. I do have a message for those in government, and that message is to work for the hard working people, and not yourselves and lazy assholes. And this country has no room for career politicians. Career politicians get cocky, arrogant, and greedy and are not good for our government. The last thing I would want to do is be President, though I think I could fix this country. There would be a lot of people who would hate me, but in the long run the country would be much better off; smaller, but much better off. The question is could you stand a dictator for four years? I would be a dictator and you would be under my hard rule of thumb for four years, and a lot of people would be deported and many would die, but in the long run we would be better off, that is, if someone didn't assassinate me. Assassination would be the most likely result, if I were to lead this country, therefore running this country is entirely out of the question. Think about this for a minute though, you know the joke about what do you call five hundred lawyers at the bottom of the ocean? Well, this would be one of the first things I would make come true, and there would be a lot of politicians going in right behind them. Well, maybe not into the ocean, but somewhere else for certain.

I do believe people have rights though, mostly those in our Bill of Rights, and eventually you would get them back with me as dictator, but first the changes need to be made to make our country great again. A dictatorship would be the best thing for our country at the moment, but I'm not talking about a ruthless, brutal, oppressive dictator. I'd be a cold hearted dictator in all likelihood, and maybe a little ruthless too. And maybe I'd be a little brutal too. Actually, I'd probably be a lot brutal. I am talking about a dictatorship that cares for the real things which really matter for people, and getting our government to the point where good, hardworking people are taken care of, not by handouts, but by allowing them to thrive through their own hard work. Lazy people on the other hand, people who refuse to learn, people who want to steal, people who burglarize homes, people who rape and plunder, and people who do the things in general which make them the scum of society, and people who are greedy and think government is only a source of handouts, would eventually be eliminated from this planet. You do not just find the scum at the bottom of the barrel; you can also find a little frothy scum at the top of the barrel too. If this would make me a murdering and brutal dictator, then so be it, but I would have the goal of making this country a better place for all who would survive. Good hard working and honest people would have no trouble sleeping at night with their doors unlocked, regardless of where they live. You certainly cannot do this today. No I am not going to become a dictator, just expressing my view of what this country needs. We need a good dictator to pull this country out of the grip of the huge monster that is cruel and vicious, not because it has the intention of being cruel and vicious, but is cruel and vicious simply because of its size and ignorance. The left hand never knows what the right hand is doing, so to speak, because of its size, and the work of getting our country going again, can only be done when both hands are working together to make it happen. One hand would have a gun in it, and the other would have a hammer.

I am a loner and I like to be left alone much of the time. I need love and a few friends and family, but most of the time I like to be alone with my work, gardening, thoughts, and care of my property and I don't interact with people any more than I need to. I have the right to do this. But on the down side, I have only one voice and one vote, when it comes to government. I choose to be this way and I do not join groups which would give me a greater voice in government, and this is my right to do so. I will never have a big voice in our government, and must depend on government doing what is right to protect my rights, and protecting my rights is their job, but government is not doing what is right for me and likely not what is right for you. Government is doing what is right for perpetuating big government, and the greedy self-centered bastards who run it, which is not what is right for me. For me, they are not doing their job.

    I feel I am getting pushed around by our government, but there is nothing I can do about this, but you come onto my property, I am the boss. I am a dictator on my property and what I say goes, and because I have and will always have the right to bear arms this will not change. I am a dictator in my little world, and this is my right. If you don't like it, well, then I suggest you stay away from me and my property. You might say I'm a little crazy. Maybe I'm a lot crazy, a real nut case and you have the right to think so, but we live in a really crazy world and maybe you have to be a little crazy to survive such a world. Hardly a week goes by where I don't kill something. There are always a few squirrels, or raccoons or something that will come around to take something which is mine and run into my shotgun. If you are a varmint as well, and come around with larceny on your mind, you may very well run into the business end of my 12-gauge shotgun too. I have never killed anyone, but never rule out this possibility.

Beware of me!

Chapter 28
Economy and Warmongering

Our country's financial condition is up and down, and this will always be the case, but if our government is doing its job, these upswings and downswings should be minimal. But it seems now our government has not only mortgaged our lives with a huge national debt, but the lives of our kids, and their kids as well. Political solutions will for the most part fail as they always do, but there is something that can be done about it. We can and should cut our military size in half, and tell every country in the world we will not fight your battles for you. Maybe if we quit pissing people off with our insatiable thirst for oil and our holier than thou attitude, we wouldn't need such a big military. Our country is really good at pissing off the people of other countries. If you are a bully, which our country is, then you have to be ready to fight constantly. We always seem to be ready to fight.

People from all over the world want to come to our country for medical care, for an education and for political and religious reasons, and this should not be allowed. I would consider letting some come here for an education if they can afford it, but very limited. When they graduate, then they go home. And why do we need to let people come over here for medical reasons? Maybe it's because we have some of the best foreign doctors over here? Maybe these guys need to go home too. There is no excuse for letting people come here for political or religious reasons. I know our country was founded on the principle of religious freedom, among others, but it is high time this is stopped. We just don't have room for more of you seeking asylum.

We still have a lot of freedom in our country compared to many countries, but every country in the world that wants what we have, can have what we have, they just need to fight for it as we have done. Every person in the world needs to own a gun and know how to use it. Governments take advantage of the weak and defenseless, more so than an armed citizenry. Brutal and oppressive dictators are brutal and oppressive, because people in these countries cannot defend themselves. But it is high time they learned to defend themselves. It is not our job to do so. We should be giving guns to the people in all the oppressed countries in the world, not fighting their battles for them. I'm sure every redneck in the US would be happy to donate a gun or two, to the people of the world in these countries. I have plenty, and I would certainly donate one or two guns to go towards arming these oppressed people. But the guns would need to go to these countries through a private group, not through our government. Our government would make it so expensive to implement such a program it would not be cost effective. Our government is so good at f_#%ing things up, it would likely f_#% this program up too.

If I had one message to give to the world, it would be, if your country is run by an oppressive and brutal leader, I say arm yourself and organize with your friends and neighbors and fight to remove your leader. Install a leader who will protect your rights. Fight and never give up! You do not need to flee your country to find a life someone else fought and died for. You owe it to yourself and you owe it to your children to fight for your rights in your own country. With today's technology, you can get hold of people online who will sell or even give you a gun. Just do it! And I would say to all the greedy, mean, oppressive, and brutal dictators and rulers of the world, there is no place for you on this planet. You cannot live off the pain and misery of others. The same is true for religious fanatics and lunatics, who only want to terrorize and destroy others in other countries and in their own country. There is no place for you on this planet, and eventually you will be destroyed. If you want to live, then live in peace and respect the rights of others. There is one simple thing most countries can do to become wealthy and happy. This is to set your country up as a fantastic vacation destination, for not just Americans, but for

<u>all</u> people of the world regardless of color, religion, or national origin. Rid your country of all who would kill or harm tourists. Give us a great deal on a fun and safe vacation, and people will flood your country and dump money on you like it was water. Care to bet on the truth of this?

I can understand why some of these rulers and fanatics are so intent on killing Americans though. The US is a very meddlesome and antagonistic country. We are and always have been war mongers. We love to fight, and have gotten to the point we have to fight for oil, to supplement our insatiable thirst for fuel to run our cars, jets, and power mowers. We are high and mighty and think our way is the only way, so we are constantly trying to force our culture upon those who maybe just don't want to listen, but we give them no choice. We will give them food, but it always comes with a sermon. I say "we" but I really mean "you" because I am not one of the "majority", and have never been in the majority.

I know our country is really messed up, and very intrusive into the affairs of many foreign countries, but I would really like to know exactly what has made them so mad, they have waged a terrorist war upon the US. What did we do to them, which is <u>so bad</u>? I do not know, and would really like to have an answer to this question. I am pissed off at our country as much as anyone, but I am not waging a terrorist war and have no intention of doing so. Well, maybe in my own way, but not through the use of explosives, bombs, or terrorist flown jets.

Making war and planning the destruction of others can't be a lot of fun. There is a lot of fun and satisfaction to be had by living in peace, and enjoying a comfortable life on a beach somewhere, and sipping a pinna colada. Playing poker at a casino, going kayaking and swimming, or visiting the Eiffel Tower has to be more fun than hiding in a cave in the mountains, and cleaning your AK-47 and worrying about whether or not today will be the day you take a bullet between the eyes, or in the back from a hungry comrade. A hot bubble bath should be preferable to hiding in the desert, fighting sand fleas and scorpions and wondering if you will ever get to take a bath again. There are deodorants in stores here which will take away the smell of your armpits you have been sniffing for a month or two, not to mention the armpits of your comrades in arms. And what did you use instead of toilet paper to clean yourself the last time you took a crap? I guarantee you the strong and soft toilet tissue I use is much better than what you used the last time you took a dump.

Life can be good, but some governments are so brutal, fighting back is necessary. These governments must give up their evil ways and learn to live in peace with their subjects; their fellow citizens. If you are the leader of one of these governments, it is time for you to change your ways or die. If you are one of his soldiers, I assure you, your brutal leader cares nothing for you. You are his pawn, and if you should die, there are others he can replace you with. Maybe you should get together with your comrades in arms and take out your leader. Say no to despotism. Choose a better life for yourself and your fellow citizens. If you choose to fight for a cruel leader, you aren't much smarter than the sand flea in your shoes, and I have no pity for you.

The President of the United States has a lot of power to steer our country in one direction or another, but the real power is in Congress. The Senate and House of Representatives control what laws get passed and which laws fail, therefore, they have the true power in the US, though the President gets the blame for most problems when things go wrong. The President with all his powers and control of the armies of the US is really just a figurehead, and cannot and should not be blamed for all the problems in this country. About the only thing the President can and should take the blame for is his war mongering. Why is it every President who is elected ends up in a war in some hellhole somewhere? Too many generals as advisors maybe, who have only one solution, and that solution will always be a military solution. Generals get retired if there is no war to fight, so their solution will always be a military one.

Presidents come and go, and little seems to change. Nothing will change as long as Congress chooses to keep things as they are. Congressmen stay in office for decades. They are the source of our problems; pompous, arrogant, and greedy career politicians. Politicians run for office because they are power hungry. They don't care about you. They are looking for a higher paying job. Some may have the intention of doing "good" for their country, and will certainly promise you great things, but inherent problems surface once they are elected. They now have a better job, and while they are still concerned with the country as a whole, their primary focus turns to their state, and what they can do for their state. They will generally toss their state a few bones in the form of "pork barrel" legislation, and always tell you they are making progress in other areas, regardless of the truth, to keep you happy. Popularity in their own state will get them re-elected, and this is job security. They must also pay back the bribes they took to get elected. The affairs of the country become secondary. It no longer matters what their legislation does to the country as a whole. When these politicians continue to get re-elected, they fall into a rut of trying to keep things as they are, while tossing a few more bones back home, as this is what is getting them re-elected. So much for doing good things for their country, they fight hardest to keep folks happy at home. And any problems that arise are always someone else's fault.

There are always newer members of Congress, who try to do "good" for their country, and even some older members of Congress who are finding their state actually expects them to be working harder for the country. But no one knows what is best for our country, and the result is congressmen do more fighting amongst themselves, rather than actually doing any good. They all have their own opinion about how things need to be done, as opinions are like assholes, everyone has one. If congressmen were limited to one term of office, and could never depend on serving in Congress as a real job, then maybe they would think a little
more about what is best for our country, and not just about

themselves and their states.

You can take this chapter and the previous chapter however you wish to take them. If you think I was trying to teach you something, then good for you. While I have always tried to teach you something throughout this book, I think I was mostly venting my disgust with our government and the world. I think a lot of people will agree with me, but then again many will not, especially those who happen to work for our government in any way, or have continually voted to keep the assholes in there; the majority. Is this a test? Maybe so; maybe no. You decide for yourself. I will explain no further.

Chapter 29
Government

The President of the United States is the head of the Executive Branch of our government. He is the commander of the armed forces. Congress, the Senate and the House of Representatives, compose the Legislative Branch, the lawmaking branch. There is another branch of the US government we hear less about. The third is the Judicial Branch, composed of the Supreme Court and numerous lower courts, and are responsible for determining whether or not laws, generated by the Legislative Branch, are constitutional. The President signs bills generated by the House and Senate to make them laws. Judges on the Supreme Court are appointed by the President and confirmed by the Senate, and serve for life. You don't hear much about this branch, and no one really knows whether or not they are doing their job, but you don't really hear much bad about the group either, so I guess they are doing okay. Well, no worse than the rest of our government. But no one really knows; at least I don't know.

The President of the US is elected by the Electoral College. You think your vote counts towards his election, and while this may be partly a contributing factor in his getting elected, the Electoral College is actually what gets him elected. There are 538 members of the Electoral College, one for each senator and representative in Congress, and three for the District of Columbia. When you vote for the President in the November election every four years, you are actually voting for Electors, who then elect the President. For the most part, the greatest number of votes from the Electoral College has elected the President, in keeping with the popular vote, your votes, but this has not always been the case. The President has been elected by the Electoral College, but has lost the election according to the popular votes by the people four times, as recently as George Bush in 2000. What I'm telling you is your vote doesn't mean squat!

I've talked mainly about our national government, but the bulk of our government includes the state and local governments as well. While there are many problems with our national government, the state and local governments comprise a much bigger portion of our total government, and they are as dysfunctional and wasteful as our national government. Every state, every county or parish, and every city has a government. Not just a little government, but much more government than we need. In my experience, local government officials are arrogant, liars and hypocrites. Local government is supposed to adhere to the same laws and regulations everyone else is forced to adhere to, but often this is not the case. Every cop, every local judge, every county commissioner, every county attorney, and the county clerk are out there, and they are out there to get you. Big brother is watching, and if you cross the line in the dirt he has drawn, he will sooner or later find you and you will be punished. You will then learn very quickly, a little more about the local judicial branch of our government. And they love snitches. Signs are posted around where I live, advising people to report poachers. Sure, there are some who will abuse our game, but living off the fat of the land they also call poaching in many cases, even if it is your own land. It is usually just a matter of paying them off (bribes), before you hunt or fish, but occasionally for not adhering to their endless list of often stupid and idiotic rules.

A case in point for our government's lying, is a series of dams built many years ago on the Guadalupe River delta where I live. Our government told the people saltwater was encroaching upon the wetlands, and when saltwater backed up into the Guadalupe River and the bayous on the delta, the saltwater was damaging the wetlands and the fisheries in the river. The gullible and naïve citizens here bought this bullshit, and the dams were built. The primary dam, called the Saltwater Barrier, was built on the Guadalupe River just below where the San Antonio River merges with the Guadalupe River, and secondary dams were built on the lower ends of several bayous just before they dump into the bay. Channels were dug so the water would flow toward the farthest dam from the Saltwater Barrier, where huge pipes were installed under the Victoria Barge Canal. These pipes were used to pump water into another channel dug. This channel ran nearly to Port Lavaca, for probably ten miles, where a water processing plant was built to purify the river water for drinking water for the city of Port Lavaca. The water is also used by some local plants along the way. Our government lied to the people to get access to a reliable source of fresh water for Port Lavaca and some of the local plants. They finally admitted they had lied, but are the dams going to be removed? Hell no! I'm not so pissed off about the dams, as for the fact they lied. Our government will lie, and do whatever is necessary, to get what they want. Screw you and everyone else. Remember, for every action, there is an equal and opposite reaction (law of physics). What helps one group of people always hurts another group of people. Take the example of lower interest rates. Lower interest helps those who want to buy and finance something. Lower interest rates hurt those who rely on interest on their money, i.e. CD's, savings accounts and money market funds. Lobbyists got us lower interest rates for real estate companies and car dealers to help them help our country grow. I rely on higher interest rates, but have no lobbyist. This is a good example of why people like me have no voice in government, and our government's "help one; screw the rest" attitude. You can't always help everyone, but when government starts screwing around with the economy, a lot of people usually end up getting hurt.

 A case in point for their arrogance is one day I was headed home and pulling my dump trailer behind my truck. I pulled into a convenience store and parked in front of a row of vacant parked cars, and out of the way of traffic. The parked cars were not hemmed in by my truck and trailer. I went in to get a soda. I came back out and got into my truck, about the same time a cop got out of his car, which was in the row of cars in front of which I had parked. Apparently, one of the cars was not vacant, but I had not noticed. He asked if I thought it was okay for me to have parked where I had parked in a cocky voice, as if there was something wrong with where I was parked. This was a public parking lot, and I had every right to park where I did, but this cop saw it a little differently. He was trying to catch speeders along the road, and I was interfering with his ability to do so, but there was in fact absolutely nothing wrong with how and where I parked. He was just pissed off because I was interfering with him and what he was doing, and he had the arrogance to confront me for doing nothing wrong but pissing him off. The asshole!

I was told by a local deputy sheriff, it is okay to drive 80 mph on the highway where the actual speed limit is 70, and I would not be ticketed for doing so. But another cop will do exactly that. Generating more business, you think? I have been ticketed for not making a complete stop at a stop sign, when cops seldom make complete stops either. You think the kettle is calling the pot black? I was driving home from work one day, and going through a neighboring town. I was pulling up to a stop light behind another car. The light was red. The car in front of me slowed, and then ran the red light. What made this incident mentionable was the license plate on the car was a government license, with "Supreme Court Judge" along the bottom. Does being a Supreme Court Judge mean he is above the law? Apparently, he thought so. I'm sure you probably have as many or more stories like this as I do. What is your opinion?

Another time I was headed to Houston and was driving up Highway 59 north, a divided freeway. I had my cruise control set at the speed limit. A car entered the freeway ahead of me and was speeding up to highway speed. I slowly caught this car and pulled up behind the vehicle within about four car lengths, and our speeds were nearly identical. I was trying to decide whether or not the vehicle would pull ahead of me, or whether I would have to pass. After a minute or so, the car did not pull ahead of me. I changed lanes and passed the car that then slowed a little. Another minute or so, a cop came up behind me and switched on his lights. I pulled over. The snotty nose little cop said I was following the vehicle I had passed too close. I tried to explain what had happened, but he would not listen and gave me a warning ticket. Looks like he should have had something a little more important to do, but no, he had to harass me a little. You might see it a little differently, especially if you happen to be in the "majority". You make the call.

Laws are one thing, but then there are regulations, those pesky little almost laws which are so rigidly enforced by local law enforcement officers. Regulations, unlike laws, are not voted on by the citizens to whom they apply, and are not produced by elected officials. They are rules devised locally and enforced locally by appointed government officials, like the regulations produced by the Texas Parks and Wildlife Department, the local despots. Don't know what despot means, well then go get a dictionary and look it up. Learn by doing which I have been so insistent on in this book. The word came up earlier. You didn't look it up then? Don't be lazy, GO LOOK IT UP!

Regulations cover every little aspect of the things you do in everyday life. Everything you do like driving your car, disposing of your trash and taking care of your kids is covered by regulations. There are rules about how you should do just about everything in your life, and if you do not do them as the government sees fit, then sooner or later you will pay the price for non-compliance. Many of these regulations are just common sense and should be easy to comply with, but just as many are just plain stupid as the people who created these regulations. Every person in this country is a criminal and is in violation of our laws, rules, or regulations. The only difference between the criminals and the non-criminals is they just haven't been caught yet. You are guilty! You still think I'm crazy? Maybe I'm still the crazy one, but I think the really nutty people run our government. So many laws and regulations are a government racket. No one knows all the laws and regulations. And you cannot know even a majority of them, because they are written in lawyer language. They don't want you to know them. This is a source of income for government, and a source of jobs to enforce (collect on) these laws and regulations. This is big business for government, and they are not about to change.

Spanking is one thing which should be mandatory for all kids. I didn't get too many spankings when I was young, but the few I did get made me a better person, especially in the 6th grade. I spanked my kids and they will tell you today, they deserved the spankings and they made them better people when they grew up. Today I would be accused of child abuse. My view is not spanking is child abuse. Not guiding children and teaching children the difference between right and wrong, and that life has penalties, will cause severe problems later. These problems are prevalent with many, many kids in the US today. I think many people will agree with me, there are a lot of problem children and young adults in the world today, but will not likely ever admit spanking will solve the problem. I beg to differ. These problems do not exist with my kids, partly because of the spankings they got. With the spankings though, there was also a generous supply of love and guidance. We never beat our kids. We spanked, guided, and loved. Kids have to learn respect, they need to learn to work, and they need to learn what things will get them into trouble or hurt them, and this cannot be done properly without spankings. At the same time, there is also a lack of guidance and love. These must also be supplied in generous portions for spankings to work well. Maybe the lack of a proper upbringing is the problem with a lot of adults these days as well.

Chapter 30
Respect

I would like to say at the outset, I have less and less respect for our government, our people, and the people of the world every day. But there is one group of people who have gained my respect recently. You might have seen the TV series Gold Rush. These guys have taken control of their lives, and while they may not be the smartest people on the planet, they are doing and learning and working very hard to make a better life for themselves. Will they succeed? Time will tell. I hope they do, and they are good examples of what I am trying to teach you. It doesn't matter how smart you are now, if you will work hard to learn the skills you need to succeed to the best of your ability, regardless of the outcome, you will gain my respect and the respect of other hard working people, who do still exist in this country, just not enough of them. If you do happen to fall, then start over again. Never give up. If you are a hard working American, and you probably know if you fit into this group, you have my respect, hands down.

Racism is little more than disrespect for people, simply because they happen to have a different gene which affects their skin color. One gene does not make the man or woman. I am racist to some extent and bigoted, and don't really care a lot for many of the people of the world, and this includes an awful lot of white folks too. I was raised in a racist society, and it is difficult to change my roots, but I do my best. I know being racist is not right, and if the people of the world are going to survive, racism must be eliminated, so I really do try my best not to be racist. I may not be totally successful all the time.

I certainly know white folks are not the only racist people in the world, and I also know there are many, many people of other countries who do not try to be otherwise. There are people who are proud of their racist ways, and often flaunt their racist habits. This cannot continue. I have run into this racism personally, and the disrespect that goes along with it, for white folks like me. We don't need so many people on this planet, because overpopulation depletes our natural resources, but we do need each other. We need to learn to live together, to work together, and if we continue to overpopulate this planet, to work together to find another place to live. We need the people who live in every country in the world; we just don't need so many of them.

Not just individual people, but religious groups, social groups and entire countries as well, exhibit racist tendencies, and all the disrespect that goes along with it. You can see this in the news every day. The Chinese have no respect for the US, as they dump their cheaply made products on the US, and we let them. They are superior, and we are a young country of brutal warmongers, in their eyes. Their only interest in the US is taking our money, and then they loan the money back to us. They laugh at us. Given half the chance, they will destroy us. They don't need armies to do this, and they know it. The Japanese do the same thing, and care nothing of the US, except as a source of money. Korea, Cambodia, Vietnam, India and many other countries have gotten in on the money train, and you can see this when you read the labels on the products you can buy. And what about the products with no labels, like crude oil and bauxite? Is it racist to think badly of these people? We let them do what they do. Do we turn the other cheek? If they continue to slap at us, do we continue to keep the cheek turned? When do we slap back?

It is said we must remember history, or else we will repeat our disasters. I remember some of history very well, and remember some of the things foreign countries have done to us over the years. Many, especially in our government, refuse to remember and will destroy this country if they do not shape up. "Remember Pearl Harbor" and "Remember the Alamo" were slogans created to help people remember, but it seems few remember anymore. Does remembering make us racist?

Does remembering the Japanese launched an unprovoked attack on Pearl Harbor, killing and maiming thousands, and disliking Japanese for this reason, make us racist? If so, then call me racist. Are we supposed to remember, or forget?

Anyone remember Hitler, the British whom we fought to get out from under their iron fist, or the Cuban missile crisis? Because we no longer remember, our country is being invaded by dozens of countries around the world, some in our own back door and others from as far away from us as you can get. This is a different kind of invasion and is crippling our economy, as they invade our country with products and take our money. But we gladly give money to them, as we have an insatiable thirst for what they have to sell, and their cheaper prices because of cheaper labor. They are happy to capitalize on this thirst. In the case of oil, they not only feed our thirst, but they also control us and have us by the balls with their greedy hands. If they would suddenly cut off our supply of oil, clothing, food, and vacation travel destinations, we would crumble. I know most people can see this happening, but there seems there is little we can do about the problem. Some are trying with alternative and renewable energy, and conservation, but not nearly enough. Why the f_#% not I'd like to know? Oh, I know. The assholes in D.C. can't do anything but argue about what is the best way to fix the problems. If they can't get together to solve the problem, then it cannot be solved, and again they all have their own opinion about what needs to be done, and no one has the same opinion.

The more I write on the subject of the problems we are facing today, the more I begin to realize our world may be doomed due to irreversible flaws. It is a big task to try to get all the people of the world to like and respect each other, rather than to just tolerate each other as many of us do now. I said earlier, it may take decades or even centuries for our world to learn to live together, to work together, and work for a common goal of producing a sustainable world. It will likely take millennia, or may not even be possible, unless one race kills off all the rest, leaving only one race of people on this planet. This probably wouldn't work either, as we are a warring people. We must love to fight, as there have been wars for all time so far. Well, at least one thing comes from fighting, population reduction. We killed most of the Indians who were living in the US, we killed an awful lot of British, and we even fought each other over the slavery issue. We want to fight, we need to fight, and most likely we will fight. The only trouble is we have the weapons of mass destruction that can destroy this planet and everyone on it. If we do not destroy ourselves, then eventually, all the natural resources will be depleted on this planet, if we continue down the same path on which we currently walk. Will we have found another planet to colonize? Don't you think we should work a little harder to find another habitable planet? We get along with the Vulcans and a few of the Ferengi and Klingons on the boob tube. You would think we could get along with some of our own species. Hell, men and women of the same color can't even get along much of the time. We're screwed!

Chapter 31
Surviving

Most of the time this little planet, the third rock from the sun, is a pretty sleepy little planet, if you don't count the vicious animals in D.C., Austin, Atlanta, Sacramento, and every other capitol in the US, and every county seat or parish in every state. It also looks very peaceful when viewed from space out of an orbiting shuttle. You would never know by looking at a photo, from just a hundred miles above the surface of the planet, such turmoil even exists, but it does and exists with a vengeance. I get up in the morning and go outside and smell the fresh air, the birds are singing, and there is very little noise and it seems there are no worries, no problems, and it is quite peaceful. Then reality sets in.

At times this little rock itself, can get almost as vicious as the politicians running this country, and the brutal leaders of other countries who rule with an iron fist, with earthquakes, drought, tornados, erupting volcanoes, hurricanes, flooding and every other severe condition which can exist on this planet. Severe weather can strike at any time, and it can strike you too. Are you ready to protect yourself from all nature can throw at you? Probably not would be my guess. No one can defend themselves from every single catastrophe which can occur 100% of the time, but if you are prepared, you will have a better chance of surviving the little things which take so many lives every year.

You can't always protect yourself from that idiot on the highway who shouldn't even be driving in the first place, but you had better be on the lookout, because he is out there, and if you are not careful he will get you. A big problem I see constantly is people seem to think an on ramp has the right of way over freeway traffic. This is absolutely not the case. Some think their blinker light gives them the right of way. This also is absolutely not true. Pay attention while driving, and learn the rules. Learn what catastrophes are most likely to affect you, and especially when you travel, what can hurt you. If you are not familiar with the area you travel to, you can be caught off guard like I was, when we were camping in the hill country west of San Antonio. You should already know most of the dangers where you live, but also learn of the dangers when you travel. This will protect you in the short term. And slow down. Why are you in such a hurry? Why do you need to get somewhere 30 seconds quicker?

There are catastrophes that can hurt you in the long term too. What if farmers were not able to produce enough food crops? What if cattle, sheep, goat, and pig ranchers were to lose a large portion or all their animals? Do you know where the next meat you eat will come from? Will you have to hunt it or catch it, and can you hunt and fish? These are good skills to know. Do you know where and when to find berries and fruits? Will you have enough water? I will, but don't count on me to tell you when, where, or how I will feed myself or supply myself with water. You must do your part if you wish to learn. If I have an excess I may share with family, but don't expect me to share with you. And certainly don't think you will take it from me. Remember my 12-gauge? If you don't know how to provide for yourself, then I think it would be a good idea for you to study where the food and water is, and how to get it.

There are wild hogs, deer, alligators, fish, some small game, and migratory animals which are plentiful around my area, and I know how to kill or catch every single one of them. I have the guns, fishing tackle, and ability to catch or kill everything I need to provide food for my needs, and I will be one of the last people on this planet to starve to death. Hell, I may not even go hungry at all with my skills. What skills do you have? Maybe it's time to learn.

And the killing is the easy part. You need to clean the food and prepare it. You will need to know how to skin a hog, deer, or whatever. You will need to know how to gut it and cut it up. And it's not over yet, there will be excess and it will need to be stored, so it does not spoil and not get contaminated. If the food you eat cannot be stored properly, you will waste a lot of food and this will make it even more difficult to provide enough food for yourself, as there will be times when you cannot catch or kill anything. You will need to survive on stored food much of the time. In the wintertime it will be easier to store food, but in the heat of summer the challenge of food storage becomes a little more difficult. Do you know how to store food? Time to learn don't you think? There are plenty of how to books on the market. Find the ones which cover the skills you need, and get started.

There are famines around the world all the time. They are mostly in Africa these days, as the population in many areas exceeds the resources, but nature deals with this through starvation, if the bleeding hearts over here will just let them alone. As the population of the planet grows and grows, there will be famine in areas you will least expect. There can be a famine here in the US, and this may currently not be too likely, but who knows what will happen next year. What would happen if all imports were to stop today? We would definitely have the ingredients for a famine right here in the good ole USA. Learn to grow your food. You will learn the food tastes better when grown to maturity on the vine, plant, or tree than what you can get in the store, and will not contain all the chemicals you will find in some of the produce delivered to stores. You will also avoid diseases which can kill you, from contaminated food grown by farmers. I don't think it's the farmer's fault so much that food contains diseases, but more from the processors and shippers of the foods. These are most likely the morons, illegals and stupid people in society, who couldn't get a really good job, because they did not study and learn what they needed to learn to get a decent job. How much do you trust these morons?

Do you assume you will always have electricity to heat and cool your home? Will you have electricity to run your freezer and refrigerator, so you can store your food? Do you assume grocery stores will always have the foods you want? What is the level of competence of the people running the water department and the gas company? I assure you those people are not the smartest people on the planet. Stop and think for a minute about all the things other people provide you to live. The people who provide you with these necessities are not concerned about your well-being. They are just doing their job, and in some cases, not doing the job very well. What if they were not able to do their job at all? If suddenly your water was cut off, and you could get no food from the grocery store, how long could you survive? If there was no gas or heating oil, how long could you last in the dead of winter? This is really something you should be thinking about, and as time goes on, you may need to think about this more and more. You should at least be thinking about this possibility now.

Also you will get the personal satisfaction you can produce your own food, and nothing can compare to that. Few people can grow and kill all their own food these days, but could you if forced to do so? The more you grow and kill for yourself now, the more skills you learn, which are needed to provide for more later, should it become necessary. How much of your own food do you provide for yourself right now? How long will it take you to get up to the point you can produce all the food you need if you started right now? Fast enough you could do so before you starve to death? The more you know now, the quicker you will be able to do so. Think about that for a minute.

There are so many different ways to prepare food, and different foods need to be prepared in different ways. If there is a catastrophe and you need to prepare your own food; grilling, baking, and boiling or steaming will be the most common ways of cooking. Learning to dehydrate foods will also be a good skill to know. If you can't even boil water now, then you are probably doomed from the start. This is not a cook book, but you will need to know how to build a fire and cook using a few spices. Spices will give you a great way to preserve and store many foods. Do you know how to smoke meat so it will keep?

Salt and black pepper are my favorite spices, and I use

them all the time, but there are others which will also be useful in the preparation of some of the tastiest meals to be had. I use a lot of garlic powder, and fresh garlic at times. There are a lot of rubs and mixed spices on the market these days, and are very good like Italian and Greek seasonings. Comino, sage, chili powder, cayenne pepper, and gumbo file (pronounced fee-lay) are also in my arsenal of spices, and I use them regularly as well. Soups and stews are easily made, and are staples around here during the winter time as is chili, but during the warmer months I like to grill my meat. I don't barbecue much, as I like the taste of meat just grilled over an open fire. I don't need the barbecue sauce, but if that is what you like, then I say go for it. I do use barbecue sauce from time to time, and it can add a little extra flavor to meat, and I mostly use barbecue sauce on pork. Everyone has different tastes, and you will find you like some things better than others, but the main thing to remember is you need to learn how to fend for yourself, and growing, killing, preparing, dehydrating, smoking and cooking is a giant step in this direction.

Guess what? It's test time again.

I am a big advocate of what?

1. Murder
2. Isolationism
3. Population control

Answer on page 197

Do I believe in God?

1. Yes
2. No

Answer on page 204

Who elects the President of the United States?

1. The Supreme Court
2. The Senate
3. The people
4. The Electoral College

Answer on page people 221

How is meat commonly preserved today?

1. Cooking
2. Smoking
3. Salting
4. Freezing

One answer on page 234 (there may be more than one correct answer)

Chapter 32
Financial Planning and Having Fun

You only get one chance at life, and as the saying goes, all work and no play makes Jack a dull boy. As much as work and learning to survive is a part of life, fun is also a big part of life. You cannot be happy if you do not have fun, and if you are not happy, you may as well not be alive. Life has to be fun, and you need to find means and methods of having a little fun along the way. This means planning your finances and being frugal at times, so you will have the resources to have fun. But if you work hard and blow all your money along the way, this will cause you a lot of problems later too. You need to learn to save for the times you wish to devote to having fun, but also provide for your current and future needs. Studying more and getting smarter, and working hard to get a better job, will help you achieve more from life, and help you more in providing for your needs. You also need to learn to save and plan for when you grow older, and will be less able to earn a living. I assure you, your government will not provide for all your future needs. A better job will help achieve this better and faster. This means learning to plan and manage your money. This also means deciding what is important to you, and not just spending to be spending; being frugal. You need to think beyond just tomorrow. You need to think about next week, next month, and next year, but you must also think ten, twenty and even forty years down the road. Poor planning will take most of your options away later, and I guarantee you will not be happy.

I worked hard most of my life, and have had fun along the way doing things with the kids like playing golf, going camping, going to the beach, and having a lot of fun around home fishing and hunting, but nothing like the fun I am having now, now that I have grown a little older. You need to plan for having fun when you get older and are not able to work as hard, and are hopefully more able financially to do things you never thought were out there, or even possible when you were younger. I never flew on a jet when I was younger, and have found I really like flying. You might too if you try it, and have never done so. I never went to foreign countries as I never flew, and found I really like going places, and learning new things about other people and cultures. I also learned more about different places in the US, though I did learn some through my history and geography studies in school, but learning up close and personal is much more fun, and what is learned is better retained. Learning by doing again as I have been preaching throughout this book.

 I do not know what fun may be for you; you will need to figure this out for yourself. What is fun for me is first living in paradise. Paradise for me is a small plot of property on the Guadalupe River along the Texas Gulf Coast, where I have access to the river and its resources, and also to the coastal bays and its resources. This area has a bountiful wildlife, where I will not likely ever have to worry about food, as I have the skills to catch this wildlife. I will never have to worry about where my next meal is coming from should disaster strike. Of course, an unnatural disaster could still hit my area head-on and destroy all life in the area, but I cannot worry about this. If this should happen, there is nothing I can do about it, and I can find another paradise elsewhere, should I be fortunate enough to survive the disaster. But in the meantime, I live in paradise. You need to find your paradise too, whatever and wherever this may be.

 It is work taking care of my place, with mowing the yard and maintaining my home, but it is also a type of fun as it is my own property I am taking care of, and there is a great deal of satisfaction which is quite rewarding in finishing a job well, like the new metal roof I recently finished. I installed the entire roof without any outside help, and this task was very rewarding. Taking care of my garden and orchard is also work, but rewarding as well. There is a great deal of personal satisfaction in nurturing tiny plants into maturity, and producing tasty and very edible foods. Is it work? Yes, but also fun.

Fun for me is also traveling with Ellen. We both love seeing new places and animals, such as the manatees in Florida, and meeting new people, but mainly doing things like kayaking and snorkeling. These are two things we love to do most. It is so peaceful to be in the water, and the myriad of creatures under the surface of the water are remarkable. Some of these creatures are quite tasty, and we do love to eat crab, shrimp, and oysters. In fact, my most favorite food is king crab, but shrimp and oysters follow close behind. I think it is so neat Ellen loves these foods as well. It is not often I find a woman who likes raw oysters as much as I do.

Playing poker online and in casinos is what I do mostly to have fun, though this is not real work at all. The long hours in the WSOP tournaments can be a bit of work however. I enjoy playing no limit hold'em, and both cash games and in tournaments of this kind. I play online numerous times a week, and when I get the chance, I like to play in Las Vegas, which I do several times a year. I enjoy online poker and I play for practice. Practice makes perfect, and I want to be able to play well enough to do well in the World Series of Poker, which is played every year at the Rio in Las Vegas, and is the largest poker tournament in the world. It consists of about 55 separate tournaments over about a month and a half, and all the best poker players from all over the world attend, to play and hopefully prove to themselves and others they are the best player on the planet. My goal is not so lofty, but I would really like to win a World Series bracelet, given out to the winners of each of the event games. The money wouldn't be too bad either, as one win could easily make you hundreds of thousands of dollars in a three-day event, to millions in the ten-day Main Event. Not a small pile of money, but I really would like to have the bracelet as much as the money; maybe next year. I am proud of my current accomplishments to date playing the best game in the world. I will continue to practice, and hopefully with a little more luck, I will get my bracelet.

    I have played poker at the Horseshoe Casino in Bossier City, Louisiana, and this is my favorite casino outside of Las Vegas to play. It is not a large casino compared to the casinos in Las Vegas, but the friendliness of the staff and the poker room, which is not all that large, is well run and one of the most fun to play at. The fact I have done very well there, could also be a factor in my liking this casino and poker room so much. Playing on a riverboat in Lake Charles, Louisiana was a bit different and fun, but not quite like playing in Bossier City. The Horseshoe Casino is also on a riverboat, but it has been modified so you can't tell it is a riverboat without going up on the roof, where I played at a recent event. They had a huge tent set up on the roof to host a WSOP Satellite Event. I have also played in Reno and Laughlin, Nevada in some small casinos, and again not that much fun compared to Las Vegas, but new learning experiences nevertheless. I have played in Tunica, Mississippi and my next new place to play will likely be in Curacao in the southern Caribbean. We'll see how this goes, although the trip to Curacao is mainly for kayaking and snorkeling. The trip will be fun no matter what, and that is what counts. The poker is secondary and doesn't really matter, as I know if I want to play some really good poker, I know where I need to go. My opinion is every poker player needs to go to Las Vegas at least once. There is no other city like it I have been to, and I doubt there ever will be another place like Las Vegas.

    My travels will never be over until I am no longer physically able to travel, but I think I will probably be pretty active until I die. I continue to work, though not as hard, and I continue to eat more things and try new things that are good for me, though I still like my beef and get withdrawal when I go too long without having a big fat beef steak. I was raised on meat and potatoes, but over especially the last few years, have learned to eat and like many foods I would never try, but I am not the man I used to be. I continue to learn to eat new things, just as I continue to learn to do new things. And I continue to learn to cook different meals and enjoy the good combinations I discover, as well as those things which don't turn out so good. If something doesn't taste good, I just keep adding and adding until it does taste good, or is at least edible. If I can't make something taste good, enough catsup to completely block out the taste will make anything taste good. Learning, doing, and having fun are the spices of life, and I will continue to do all three, especially the fun things, until the day I die.

Epilogue

I wrote this book for one reason initially, and this was to try to teach you a few things you really should know in life. I also wanted to show you how to live a better life, be really happy and have some fun along the way, but in teaching you some of the things you should know I did not want this book to be a textbook. I am happy with how I have lived my life, and I think my life has been pretty interesting, so I also made this book about my life. Of course, there was a generous supply of sarcasm, and I also wanted it to be humorous at times and be fun to read, with a lot of little stories about myself, my family and some of the things I have done along the road of life, you never thought of doing yourself. I don't know how humorous the book has been for you, but at least I tried.

I also wanted to help you achieve more in life, and to help you pick yourself up and move forward to a better life, regardless of your current shape. I wanted to help give you the inner strength, the mental strength to work towards a better life. Again, I don't know how well I did this, but I tried. I truly believe if there were more people like me, the world would be a much better place. I have the strength to endure, and not let problems interfere with my life. How about you?

If I can help you live a better life and feel better about yourself, then I have accomplished my task. Hopefully you are a little bit smarter now than you were before. If you really want to learn and live a better life, then this book will not be the last you read, and you will begin to do more in life and with your life. If not, then stay stupid because to tell you the truth, I really don't care and just reading this book is not nearly enough to make you smart, it is only a primer. If you do not change your life starting right now, you will not gain the success I have tried to get you on your way to achieving, so if you want to be a lazy ass, hopefully you will die soon enough, if the bleeding hearts can stay away from your door. The world of the future does not have a place for those who do not exert the necessary mental and physical force to be the best they can be. Just remember, I think there are too many people on this planet. If you are content to be a lazy, stupid or dumb person, I really hope you die, and the sooner the better.

I would not change a single thing that has ever happened in my life. I know everything that has happened in my life, has made me a better and stronger person. There are a few things I regret, but to change the past would change me, and I really like who I am, where I am at, and where I am going. I am strong mentally and physically, and though I get a little bored from time to time, I do not stay bored as long as I have short term and long term plans and goals. I cannot take the summer heat outside I could take when I was younger, but there is nothing I can do about this. Also, I do not have the durability I had when I was younger, but outside of this, there are few limits to what I can do.

No matter what you learn in this book and in life, you need to learn what things you can change and what you cannot, and stay away from those things you cannot change. Concentrate on your life and those things which affect your life, and don't try to change things you cannot change. You always need to be optimistic, and don't let things get you down. Everyone does something stupid from time to time, but many people can't seem to do much that is not stupid. Stop for a minute and think about what you are doing, and maybe you will do less stupid stuff, and maybe the life you save will not be just yours, but mine as well.

You are made of water, minerals, and organic chemicals and how you feel is largely related to what you eat and what you breathe. All people on this planet are responsible for the pollutants you breathe, and for the present time you cannot do much about this, but hopefully eventually, maybe the planetary population will go down and you will breathe a little easier and healthier. If you are sniffing stuff you really should not be sniffing, and you know what I'm talking about, to just get high or something, then I hope whatever it is kills you. You are stupid and really should die. Now!

What you can easily control though, is what and how much you eat. When you eat something, you start a chemical reaction, and these chemicals will affect how you feel and how you act. Think about that. Also, eating too much is just asking for problems, if you are eating so much you get really fat. A fat slob is just asking for trouble, and I hope you either lose the weight, or die, which you probably will, just not soon enough to suit me. I like food and how it tastes as much as the next person, but it does not control my life. I am a bit overweight and will always be a little overweight, but I am not a fat slob and am very comfortable with my weight. If you are fat and want to lose weight, then just lose it. You don't need to be skinny, just not a fat slob where you have a serious problem walking, working and enjoying life. This is all about mental strength, something you will need to survive. If you don't have the mental strength to lose the weight, then you don't have the mental strength for life in the future, and I hope you die soon and put yourself out of your misery. You are just a waste of space.

Okay, let's have one final test. Let's see if you are still the same dumb jackass you were when you started this book. I included several tests in this book for you to self-check your progress with your learning. How well did you do with the tests? You do not have to answer this question; the tests were completely for you. Another test now, you say? Nah, you don't need another stinkin' test. The real test is you, and what you do with your life the next two or three years. I will not judge you on this test either. You must learn to test yourself and question your progress. Did you absorb much of what I was trying to teach you with my book? Will you get off your ass and try to learn more? Will you get into shape so you can do the work you need to do to survive, and also be in good shape to have more fun out of life? I have tried to entertain you, but more importantly I have tried to motivate you to become smarter, to do less stupid stunts, to take charge of your life and study harder, and tried to help you become mentally stronger, so you can deal with life's challenges. I hope I was successful. The next few years will tell the story. I wish you the best of luck if you put forth the effort. If you do not put forth the effort, then you probably know me well enough by now, to know what I want you to do. Thank you for reading my book.

THE END

About the Author

A lifelong native of the Guadalupe River Delta on the Texas Gulf Coast, Larry Landgraf worked first as a commercial fisherman, then as a general contractor before severe injury led to his career as an author. He wrote one book before *Smart SOB*, then followed those with his epic Four Seasons series. The father of three grown children, Larry brought his beloved city-gal Ellen to the Delta in 2009. Now he teaches her the ways of his swamp, and she teaches him more than he ever imagined.

Fresh Ink Group

Publishing
Free Memberships
Share & Read Free Stories, Essays, Articles
Free-Story Newsletter
Writing Contests

Books
E-books
Amazon Bookstore

Authors
Editors
Artists
Professionals
Publishing Services
Publisher Resources

Members' Websites
Members' Blogs
Social Media

www.FreshInkGroup.com
Email: info@FreshInkGroup.com
Twitter: @FreshInkGroup
Google+: Fresh Ink Group
Facebook.com/FreshInkGroup
LinkedIn: Fresh Ink Group
About.me/FreshInkGroup

INTO AUTUMN
A Story of Survival

By Larry Landgraf

Lars is living alone in the Texas countryside when the economy collapses and his world becomes a dystopian nightmare. Joined by outsider Eileen, he and his neighbors band together for survival in their "Peaceful Valley." They must learn to scratch out sustenance while fending off predatory invasions in an increasingly violent and lethal world. *Into Autumn* is a sweeping adventure, a thought-provoking saga that could happen to us all.

www.FreshInkGroup.com

Paper-cover ISBN-13: 978-1-936442-54-6
Hardcover ISBN-13: 978-1-936442-53-9
Ebook ISBN-13: 978-1-936442-55-3

INTO SPRING
The Next Generation

By Larry Landgraf

Twenty years after *Into Autumn*, Sean and Robbie leave Peaceful Valley for Corpus Christi, hoping to find women who will join their fiercely protective group back home. What they find is a fight to survive the violent dictatorship of ruthless Sandra Hawkins. Meanwhile, a new family joins the group in the Valley, except that what seems like a safe addition might bring the worst kinds of change. *Into Spring* continues the Four Seasons saga about building a new life in Texas after the collapse of civilization.

www.FreshInkGroup.com
Paper-cover ISBN-13: 978-1-936442-44-7
Hardcover ISBN-13: 978-1-936442-43-0
Ebook ISBN-13: 978-1-936442-45-4